Seferim Khanok
Books of Enoch

Translated By Rabbi Simon Altaf
Translation 2nd Nov 2010 African-Israel International
Second Edition

African-Israel International Y'sra'elite Qahalim 2010

Revised: 18, Feb 2015

Excerpts can be used from this book outside modification for study or reprinting purposes with the set condition that as long as reference is given back to the author and this true names book for any commentary or text taken out.

Rebbe Simon Altaf; email: shimoun63@yahoo.com
Rebbe Lamont Clophus, African-Israel, 8111 Mainland, Suite 104-152, San Antonio, Texas, 78240, USA

To contact us via e-mail through africanysrael@yahoo.com or phone Rebbe Lamont in the USA: Tel 1-210-827-3907.

Seferim Khanok

Gulf: Rabbi John 971 244 63 617

Philippines: Rabbi Robert: 63-908-444-2866

North America Chief Rabbi: Rabbi Kefa Ben Yahudah
Tel: 1-210-827-3907

Visit our website at: www.african-israel.com;

All quotes are from the Hidden Truths Hebraic Scroll (HTHS) unless otherwise stated

From the translation of the Ethiopic text by Richard Laurence,
London, 1883.
Two Khanok translated from the Slavonic by W. R. Morfill, M.A.
Three Khanok by R. Yshma'el Ben Elisha

Seferim Khanok

Preface

These books are proposed to be of Khanok the son of Yered. They are placed in the timeline of around 2nd century BC however one thing is certain that changes may have been made to these books by later authors of unknown origin. The second thing is certain that Khanok was living in what today is called the African Continent such as central Nigeria. Khanok was our black African forefather of priestly clan who shared ancestry with Qayin and Sheth. These priestly clans married two wives usually and kept them in the North/South Axis. One wife from the father's side and the second from the mother's side a paternal cousin/niece and a maternal cousin. The firstborn son was named after the patrilineal wife's father or grandfather such as Abraham's wife Keturah named her firstborn son Jokshan after Joktan the father of Keturah. Keturah was Abraham's second wife placed in the south in Beersheba while Abraham was living in the North with his wife Sarah, Abraham including Sarah and Keturah were people of colour what would be described as Negro looking today. They shared ancestry with Ham and Shem both being black. See Hidden-Truths Hebraic Scrolls Complete bible www.african-israel.com. The translation of the KJV and JPS bibles is at fault in Genesis 25:1 which makes it appear like Abraham took Keturah as wife after Sarah's death. See the HTHS corrected translation.

They kept many customs of ritual purity and even did animal sacrifices to Elohim for blood guilt. We find this did happen with Abraham who is from the same ancestry in Genesis 14:18 when Shem shows up to do the increases and blood guilt sacrifices for the war that Abraham had just fought. This is still common in some Asian cultures today. In the Muslim culture of Pakistan when people seem to be struggling or believe they have done something wrong they bring a black goat or lamb for a blood guilt sacrifice so that all their sins will transfer unto the goat and the affect of any guilt will fall on the animal.

The land of Nok was the central area of modern Nigeria three hundred miles along the Benue River rising across northern Cameroon and traversing through Eastern Central Nigeria merging into the Niger river where these people were both agriculturists and metal workers also known later as the Yoruba. Note Qayin killed his brother Hebel with a metal instrument since he was a metal worker (Gen 4:8)

They introduced iron to the surrounding Africans with their special Iron smelting process. This culture seems to have disappeared around 500 CE. The area of Bor-nu (Land of Noakh) not far from this region was a known landing place of the Ark of Noakh after the flood. The Nok culture was discovered by an English man by the name of Lt-Colonel John Dent-Young near the Jos Plateau. What is not known by many that the term Nok and Nod where Qayin went (Gen 4:16) and are synonymous terms..

Seferim Khanok
First Book of Chanok

- Preface *3*
- Chapter 1 .... *11*
- Chapter 2 .... *12*
- Chapter 3 .... *12*
- Chapter 4 .... *12*
- Chapter 5 .... *12*
- Chapter 6 .... *12*
- Chapter 7 .... *14*
- Chapter 8 .... *16*
- Chapter 9 .... *16*
- Chapter 10 .... *18*
- Chapter 11 does not exist *21*
- Chapter 12 .... *21*
- Chapter 13 .... *22*
- Chapter 14 .... *23*
- Chapter 15 .... *26*
- Chapter 16 .... *27*
- Chapter 17 .... *28*
- Chapter 18 .... *28*
- Chapter 19 .... *30*
- Chapter 20 .... *31*
- Chapter 21 .... *31*
- Chapter 22 .... *32*
- Chapter 23 .... *34*
- Chapter 24 .... *34*
- Chapter 25 .... *36*
- Chapter 26 .... *36*
- Chapter 27 .... *37*
- Chapter 28 .... *37*
- Chapter 29 .... *37*
- Chapter 30 .... *38*

Seferim Khanok

Chapter 31 38

Chapter 32 39

Chapter 33 39

Chapter 34 39

Chapter 35 40

Chapter 36 does not exist 40

Chapter 37 40

Chapter 38 41

Chapter 39 42

Chapter 40 43

Chapter 41 44

Chapter 42 45

Chapter 43 45

Chapter 44 46

Chapter 45 46

Chapter 46 47

Chapter 47 48

Chapter 48 48

Chapter 48A 50

Chapter 49 50

Chapter 50 51

Chapter 51 51

Chapter 52 52

Chapter 53 53

Chapter 54 54

Chapter 55 55

Chapter 56 56

Chapter 57 57

Chapter 58 57

Chapter 59 59

Chapter 60 60

Chapter 61 62

Seferim Khanok

Chapter 62 64
Chapter 63 66
Chapter 64 66
Chapter 65 67
Chapter 66 68
Chapter 67 69
Chapter 68 70
Chapter 69 74
Chapter 70 74
Chapter 71 76
Chapter 72 81
Chapter 73 82
Chapter 74 83
Chapter 75 85
Chapter 76 86
Chapter 77 87
Chapter 78 89
Chapter 79 90
Chapter 80 92
Chapter 81 93
Chapter 82 96
Chapter 83 97
Chapter 84 98
Chapter 85 99
Chapter 86 100
Chapter 87 101
Chapter 88 101
Chapter 89 112
Chapter 90 117
Chapter 91 118
Chapter 92 119
Chapter 93 122

Seferim Khanok

Chapter 94 123

Chapter 95 123

Chapter 96 124

Chapter 97 127

Chapter 98 128

Chapter 99 129

Chapter 100 130

Chapter 101 missing 131

Chapter 102 131

Chapter 103 132

Chapter 104 134

Chapter 104A 135

Chapter 105 136

End of 1 KhanokThe scroll of the Secrets of Khanok 145

The scroll of the Secrets of Khanok 146

Chapter 1 146

Chapter 2 147

Chapter 3 147

Chapter 4 147

Chapter 5 147

Chapter 6 148

Chapter 7 148

Chapter 8 148

Chapter 9 149

Chapter 10 149

Chapter 11 151

Chapter 12 151

Chapter 13 151

Chapter 14 152

Chapter 15 152

Chapter 16 153

Chapter 17	154
Chapter 18	154
Chapter 19	155
Chapter 20	155
Chapter 21	156
Chapter 22	157
Chapter 23	158
Chapter 24	159
Chapter 25	159
Chapter 26	160
Chapter 27	160
Chapter 28	161
Chapter 29	161
Chapter 30	162
Chapter 31	163
Chapter 32	164
Chapter 33	164
Chapter 34	166
Chapter 35	167
Chapter 36	167
Chapter 37	167
Chapter 38	167
Chapter 39	168
Chapter 40	168
Chapter 41	170
Chapter 42	170
Chapter 43	170
Chapter 44	171
Chapter 45	171
Chapter 46	171
Chapter 47	172
Chapter 48	172

Chapter 49 173
Chapter 50 174
Chapter 51 174
Chapter 52 175
Chapter 53 177
Chapter 54 177
Chapter 55 177
Chapter 56 177
Chapter 57 178
Chapter 58 178
Chapter 59 179
Chapter 60 179
Chapter 61 179
Chapter 62 180
Chapter 63 180
Chapter 64 180
Chapter 65 181
Chapter 66 182
Chapter 67 183
Chapter 68 183

The scroll of Three Khanok 3 Khanok 185
Chapter 1 185
Chapter 2 187
Chapter 3 187
Chapter 4 187
Chapter 5 189
Chapter 6 192
Chapter 7 192

The End of the scroll of fragments. 193

.Glossary 193

Glossary 194

Seferim Khanok

Chapter 1

1 The word of the increases of Khanok, how he consecrated the elect and the tsadik, who were to exist in the time of trouble; rejecting all the evildoers and wicked. Khanok, a tsadik man, who *was*[1] with Elohim, answered and spoke, while his eyes were open, and *while* he saw a set-apart vision in the shamayim. This malakhim showed me.

2 From them I heard all things, and understood what I saw; that which will not take place in this generation, but in a generation which is to succeed at a distant period,[2] on account of the elect.[3]

3 Upon their account I spoke and conversed with him, who will go forth from his habitation, the Set-apart and Mighty One, the Elohim of the world:

4 Who will hereafter tread upon Mount Siniyah; appear with his hosts; and be manifested in the strength of his power from shamayim.

5 All shall be afraid, and the Watchers[4] be terrified.

6 Great fear and trembling shall seize them, even to the ends of the eretz. The lofty mountains shall be troubled, and the exalted hills depressed, melting like a honeycomb in the flame. The eretz shall be immerged, and all things which are in it perish; while judgment shall come upon all, even upon all the tsadik:

7 But to them shall he give shalom: he shall preserve the elect, and towards them exercise clemency.

8 Then shall all belong to Elohim; be happy and increased; and the splendor of the majesty shall illuminate them.

---

[1] The italicized words supply a gap in the text.
[2] End-Times.
[3] Y'sra'el
[4] Special guardian heavenly messengers.

Seferim Khanok

Chapter 2
1 Behold, he comes with ten thousands of his kedushim to execute judgment upon them, and destroy the wicked, and reprove all the carnal for everything which the sinful and evildoers have done, and committed against him.[1]

Chapter 3
1 All who are in the shamayim know what is established *there*.

2 *They know* that the heavenly luminaries change not their paths; that each rises and sets regularly, every one at its proper period, without transgressing the commands, *which they have received*. They behold the eretz and understand what is there established from the beginning to the end of it.

3 *They see* that every work of Elohim is invariable in the period of its appearance. They behold summer and winter: *perceiving* that the whole eretz is full of mayim; and that the cloud, the dew, and the rain refresh it.

Chapter 4
1 They consider and behold every etz, how it appears to wither, and every leaf to fall off, except of fourteen etzim, which are not deciduous; which wait from the ancient times, to the appearance of the new *leaf*, for two or three winters.

Chapter 5
1 Again they consider the days of summer, that the sun is upon it at its very beginning; while you seek for a covered and shady spot on account of the burning sun; while the eretz is scorched up with fervid heat, and you become incapable of walking either upon the ground or upon the rocks in consequence of that heat.

Chapter 6
1 They consider how the etzim, when they put forth their green leaves, become covered, and produce fruit; understanding everything, and knowing that He who lives forever does all these things for you:

---

[1] Jude quoted in similar fashion.

Seferim Khanok

2 *That* the works at the beginning of every existing year, that all his works, are subservient to him, and invariable; yet as Elohim has appointed, so are all things brought to pass.

3 They see, too, how the seas and the rivers together complete their respective operations:

4 *But* you endure not patiently, nor fulfill the commandments of YHWH; but you transgress and calumniate *his* greatness; and malignant are the words in your polluted mouths against his Majesty.

5 You withered in heart, no shalom shall be to you!

6 Therefore your days shall you curse, and the years of your lives shall perish; perpetual execration shall be multiplied, and you shall not obtain mercy.

7 In those days shall you resign your shalom with the eternal maledictions of all the tsadik and transgressors shall perpetually execrate you;

8 *Shall execrate* you with the evildoers.

9 The elect shall possess light, joy, and shalom; and they shall inherit the eretz.

10 But you, wicked one's, shall be accursed.

11 Then shall wisdom[1] be given to the elect, all of whom shall live, and not again transgress by impiety or pride; but shall humble themselves, possessing prudence, and shall not repeat transgression.

12 They shall not be condemned the whole period of their lives, not die in torment and indignation; but the sum of their days shall be completed, and they shall grow old in shalom; while the years of their happiness shall be

---

[1] The mother chochmah known as the Holy Spirit is the feminine trait of Ab YHWH.

Seferim Khanok

multiplied with joy, and with shalom, forever, the whole duration of their existence.

Chapter 7
1 It happened after the sons of men had multiplied in those days that daughters were born to them, elegant and beautiful.

2 And when the watchers in Shamayim,[1] the sons of shamayim, beheld them, they became enamoured of them, saying to each other, come, let us select for ourselves wives from the progeny of men, and let us beget children.[2]

3 Then their leader Shemyaza[3] said to them; I fear that you may perhaps be indisposed to the performance of this enterprise;

4 And that I alone shall suffer for so grievous a crime.

5 But they answered him and said, we all swear;[4]

6 And bind ourselves by mutual curses,[5] that we will not change our intention, but execute our projected undertaking.

7 Then they swore all together, and all bound themselves by mutual execrations. Their whole number was two hundred, who descended upon Ardis, which is the top of mount Hermon.[6]

---

[1] Guardian Angels
[2] Some angels appear to have the ability to procreate but the procreation with women will only bring about children malformed in various ways because that is not their design.
[3] Lilith's adulterous husband to throw down mankind, their son was Azazel see Lev 16:8. also see Gen 1:27 and 3:1 in the HTHS Study bible.
[4] This oath took place on Mount Herman in Israel.
[5] The curses and oath to destroy mankind that Shaitan had decided before he fell.
[6] Mount Herman.

Seferim Khanok

8 That mountain therefore was called Hermon,[1] because they had sworn upon it and bound themselves by mutual curses.

9 These are the names of their chiefs: Shemyaza, who was their leader, Urakabarameel, Akibeel, Tamiel, Ramuel, Daniel, Azkeel, Saraknyal, Asael, Armers, Batraal, Anane, Zavebe, Samsaveel, Ertael, Turiel, Yomiel, Arazyal. These were the prefects of the two hundred malakhim, and the remainder were all with them.

10 Then they took wives, each choosing for himself; whom they began to approach, and with whom they cohabited; teaching them sorcery, incantations, and the dividing of roots[2] and etzim.[3]

11 And the women conceiving brought forth giants. [And they *the women* bore to them *the Watchers* three races first, the great giants. The giants slew the Naphelim, and the Naphelim slew the Elioud. And they existed, increasing in power according to their greatness.][4]

12 Whose stature was each three hundred cubits. These devoured all *which* the labor of men *produced;* until it became impossible to feed them;

13 When they turned themselves against men, in order to devour them;

14 And began to injure birds, beasts, reptiles, and fishes, to eat their flesh one after another, and to drink their blood.[5]

15 Then the eretz reproved the unruly.

---

[1] Herman is derived from the ancient Hebrew word Herem for curse.
[2] Used plants for evil purposes.
[3] This is why we find a lot of women into witchcraft because they were the first recipients of the information from the watchers.
[4] The bracketed is extra text in one of the Greek Ethiopic text.
[5] These class of giants that were huge started also to destroy each other alongside birds and animals. They did exist and this is not a legend we have remains of very large giant that the world does not want to talk about. Search for it you will find pictures of them on the internet.

Seferim Khanok

Chapter 8

1 Moreover Azazyel[1] taught men to make swords, knives, shields, breastplates, the fabrication of mirrors, and the workmanship of bracelets and ornaments, the use of paint, the beautifying of the eyebrows, *the use of* stones of every valuable and select kind, and all sorts of dyes, so that the world became altered.[2]

2 Impiety increased; whoring multiplied; and they transgressed and corrupted all their ways.

3 Amazarak taught all the sorcerers, and dividers of roots:

4 Armers *taught* the solution of sorcery;

5 Barkayal *taught* the observers of the stars,[3]

6 Akibeel *taught* signs;

7 Tamiel taught astronomy;

8 And Asaradel taught the motion of the moon,

9 And men, being destroyed, cried out; and their voice reached to shamayim.

Chapter 9

1 Then Micha'el and Gabri'el, Raphael, Suryal, and Uri'el,[4] looked down from shamayim, and saw the quantity of blood which was shed on eretz, and all the iniquity which was done upon it, and said one to another, *It is* the voice of their cries;

---

[1] The son of Lilith Adam's first wife and the adultery between Samyaza. The goat is sent in his remembrance in Lev 16:8 to remember the first evil woman that fell. Many women are acting out the Lilith today.
[2] All these arts were taught by rebellious angels to men and women both.
[3] In modern day termed astrology but ancient astrology was not just about future forecast but also how to chart your present distance in journeys from one place to another.
[4] Five of the archangels.

Seferim Khanok

2 The eretz deprived *of her children* has cried even to the gate of shamayim.[1]

3 And now to you, O you set-apart one of shamayim, the souls of men complain, saying, Obtain Justice[2] for us with the Most High. Then they said to YHWH, the King, *You are* Master of masters, the super power above all powers, King of kings. The throne of your esteem is forever and ever, and forever and ever is your name sanctified and esteemed. You are Benevolent and esteemed.

4 You have made all things; you possess power over all things; and all things are open and manifest before you. You behold all things, and nothing can be concealed from you.

5 You have seen what Azazyel has done, how he has taught every species of iniquity upon eretz, and has disclosed to the world all the secret things which are done in the shamayim.

6 Shemyaza also has taught sorcery to whom you have given authority over those who are associated with him. They have gone together to the daughters of men; have lain with them; have become polluted;

7 And have revealed these transgressions.

8 The women likewise have brought forth giants.

9 Thus has the whole eretz been filled with blood and with iniquity.

10 And now behold the souls of those who are dead, cry out.

11 And complain even to the gate of shamayim.

---

[1] When men cry down here due to transgression the voices are heard by shamayim.
[2] Hebraically it means to cast judgment upon the earth for its rebellion and murder.

Seferim Khanok

12 Their groaning ascends; nor can they escape from the unrighteousness which is committed on eretz. You know all things, before they exist.

13 You know these things, and what has been done by them; yet you do not speak to us.

14 What on account of these things ought we to do to them?

Chapter 10
1 Then the Most High, the Great and Set-apart One spoke,

2 And sent Arsayalalyur[1] to the son of Lamakh,

3 Saying, say to him in my name conceal yourself.

4 Then explain to him the consummation which is about to take place; for all the eretz shall perish; the waters of a deluge[2] shall come over the whole eretz, and all things which are in it shall be destroyed.

5 And now teach him how he may escape, and how his seed may remain in all the eretz.

6 Again YHWH said to Raphael, bind Azazyel hand and foot; cast him into darkness; and opening the desert which is in Dudael,[3] cast him in there.

7 Throw upon him hurled and pointed stones,[4] covering him with darkness;

8 There shall he remain forever;[1] cover his face, that he may not see the light.[2]

---

[1] One Greek text reads Uriel.
[2] The action of these watchers brought the flood so to destroy mankind and start with one right-ruling family of Noach.
[3] Area in Saudi Arabia where some of these angels are bound in She'ol in a section reserved for them.
[4] Punishing him with special stones piercing him that have a painful effect on angels.

Seferim Khanok

9 And in Yom Ha Din³ let him be cast into the fire.⁴

10 Restore the eretz, which the malakhim have corrupted; and announce life to it, that I may revive it.

11 All the sons of men shall not perish in consequence of every secret, by which the Watchers have destroyed, and *which* they have taught, their offspring.

12 All the eretz has been corrupted by the effects of the teaching of Azazyel.⁵ To him therefore ascribe the whole crime.

13 To Gabri'el also YHWH said, go to the mumzair,⁶ to the reprobates, to the children of whoring; and destroy the children of whoring, the offspring of the Watchers, from among men; bring them forth, and excite them one against another. Let them perish by *mutual* slaughter; for length of days shall not be theirs.

14 They shall all entreat you, but their fathers shall not obtain *their wishes* respecting them; for they shall hope for eternal life, and that they may live, each of them, five hundred years.

15 To Micha'el likewise YHWH said, go and announce *his crime* to Shemyaza, and to the others who are with him, who have been associated with women, that they might be polluted with all their impurity. And when all their sons shall be slain, when they shall see the perdition of their beloved, bind them for seventy generations underneath the eretz,⁷ even to the Day of Judgment, and of consummation, until

---

¹ Forever here refers to until they are thrown into the lake of fire in the end.
² A special cloth from shamayim to cover his eyes that he cannot see.
³ Great day of judgment.
⁴ Lake of sulphur.
⁵ The chief architect of this crime. Remember the scapegoat or Azazel (Lev 16:8) that was sent. That was to remember what had happened here and to cast sin outside the camp.
⁶ Hybrid or Bastards in Hebrew.
⁷ In the regions of Saudi Arabia for 7000 years, each generation to be 100 years each. Then follow with 3000 years equals 10,000 years before they will be thrown into the lake of fire.

the judgment, *the effect of* which will last for ever, be completed.

16 Then shall they be taken away into the lowest depths of the fire in torments; and in confinement shall they be shut up forever.

17 Immediately after this shall Shemyaza together with them, burn and perish; they shall be bound until the consummation of many generations.

18 Destroy all the souls addicted to lust and the offspring of the Watchers, for they have tyrannized over mankind.

19 Let every oppressor perish from the face of the eretz;

20 Let every evil work be destroyed;

21 The plant of right-ruling and of rectitude appear and its produce become an increase.

22 Right-ruling and rectitude shall be for ever planted with delight.

23 And then shall all the kedushim give thanks, and live until they have begotten a thousand *children*,[1] while the whole period of their youth, and their Sabbaths shall be completed in shalom. In those days all the eretz shall be cultivated in right-ruling; it shall be wholly planted with etzim, and filled with benediction; every etz of delight shall be planted in it.

24 In it shall vines be planted; and the vine which shall be planted in it shall yield fruit to satiety; every seed, which shall be sown in it, shall produce for one measure a thousand; and one measure of olives shall produce ten presses of oil.

---

[1] One child counted for each day of the millennial reign.

Seferim Khanok

25 Purify the eretz from all oppression,[1] from all injustice, from all crime, from all impiety, and from all the pollution which is committed upon it exterminate them from the eretz.

26 Then shall all the children of men be tsadik, and all nations shall pay me divine honour, and exalt me; and all shall adore me.

27 The eretz shall be cleansed from all corruption, from every crime, from all punishment, and from all suffering; neither will I again send a deluge upon it from generation to generation for ever.

28 In those days I will open the treasures of increases which are in shamayim, that I may cause them to descend upon eretz, and upon all the works and labour of man.

29 Shalom and equity shall associate with the sons of men all the days of the world, in every generation of it.

Chapter 11 does not exist

Chapter 12

1 Before all these things Khanok was concealed; nor did any one of the sons of men know where he was concealed, where he had been, and what had happened.

2 He was wholly engaged with the set-apart ones and with the Watchers in his days.

3 I Khanok, was magnifying the great Master and King of Shalom.[2]

4 And behold the Watchers called me Khanok the scribe.

5 Then *the Master* said to me: Khanok, scribe of right-ruling, go tell the Watchers of shamayim, who have

---

[1] The earth was going to receive a mikvah (baptism) through the flood cleansing its impurities e.g. people.
[2] See Hidden-Truths Hebraic Scrolls Isaiah 9:6.

Seferim Khanok

deserted the lofty sky, and their set-apart everlasting station,[1] *who* have been polluted with women.

6 And have done as the sons of men do, by taking to themselves wives, and *who* have been greatly corrupted on the eretz;

7 That on the eretz they shall never obtain shalom and remission of transgression. For they shall not rejoice in their offspring; they shall behold the slaughter of their beloved; shall lament for the destruction of their sons; and shall petition for ever; but shall not obtain mercy and shalom.

Chapter 13

1 Then Khanok, passing on, said to Azazyel: You shall not obtain shalom. A great sentence is gone forth against you. He shall bind you;

2 Neither shall relief, mercy, and supplication be yours, on account of the oppression which you have taught;

3 And on account of every act of blasphemy, tyranny, and transgression, which you have discovered to the children of men.

4 Then departing *from him* I spoke to them all together;

5 And they all became terrified, and trembled;

6 Beseeching me to write for them a memorial of supplication, that they might obtain forgiveness; and that I might make the memorial of their petition ascend up before the Elohim of shamayim; because they could not themselves thence forwards address him, nor raise up their eyes to shamayim on account of the disgraceful offence for which they were judged.

7 Then I wrote a memorial of their petition and supplications, for their ruakh, for everything which they had

---

[1] Their appointed jobs.

Seferim Khanok

done, and for the subject of their entreaty, that they might obtain remission and rest.

8 Proceeding on, I continued over the waters of Danbadan, which is on the right to the west of Hermon[1] reading the memorial of their petition, until I fell asleep.

9 And behold a dream came to me, and visions appeared above me. I fell down and saw a vision of punishment, that I might relate it to the sons of shamayim, and reprove them. When I awoke I went to them. All being collected together stood weeping in Oubelseyael, which is situated between Libanos and Seneser,[2] with their faces veiled.

10 I related in their presence all the visions which I had seen, and my dream;

11 And began to utter these words of right-ruling, reproving the Watchers of shamayim.

Chapter 14
1 This is the book of the words of right-ruling, and of the reproof of the Watchers, who belong to the world, according to that which He, who is set-apart and great, commanded in the vision. I perceived in my dream that I was now speaking with a tongue of flesh, and with my breath, which the Mighty One has put into the mouth of men, that they might converse with it.

2 And understand with the heart. As he has created and given to men *the power of* comprehending the word of understanding, so has he created and given to me *the power of* reproving the Watchers, the offspring of shamayim. I have written your petition; and in my vision it has been shown me, that what you request will not be granted you as long as the world endures.

---

[1] Mediterranean.
[2] Lebanon and Damascus.

Seferim Khanok

3 Judgment has been passed upon you: *your request* will not be granted you.[1]

4 From this time forward, never shall you ascend into shamayim; He has said that on the eretz He will bind you, as long as the world endures.[2]

5 But before these things you shall behold the destruction of your beloved sons; you shall not possess them, but they shall fall before you by the sword.

6 Neither shall you entreat for them, not for yourselves;

7 But despite your tears and prayers you will receive nothing. The words of the writings which I have written.

8 A vision thus appeared to me.

9 Behold, in *that* vision clouds and a mist invited me; agitated stars and flashes of lightning impelled and pressed me forwards, while winds in the vision assisted my flight, accelerating my progress.

10 They elevated me aloft to shamayim. I proceeded, until I arrived at a wall built with stones of crystal. A tongue of fire surrounded it, which began to strike me with terror.[3]

11 Into this tongue of fire I entered;

12 And drew near to a spacious habitation built also with stones of crystal. Its walls too, as well as pavement, were *formed* with stones of crystal, and crystal likewise was the ground. Its roof had the appearance of agitated stars and flashes of lightning; and among them were cherubim of fire in the shamayim of mayim. A flame burned around its walls; and its portal blazed with fire. When I entered into this dwelling, it was hot as fire and cold as ice. No *trace* of delight or of life was there. Terror overwhelmed me, and a fearful shaking seized me.

---

[1] Once YHWH passes judgment there is no change in it.
[2] 10,000 years before the world is renewed.
[3] This is astral travel.

Seferim Khanok

13 Violently agitated and trembling, I fell upon my face. In the vision I looked.

14 And behold there was another habitation more spacious than *the former*, every entrance to which was open before me, erected in *the midst of* a vibrating flame.

15 So greatly did it excel in all points, in esteem, in magnificence, and in magnitude, that it is impossible to describe to you either the splendor or the extent of it.

16 Its floor was on fire; above were lightnings and agitated stars, while its roof exhibited a blazing fire.

17 Attentively I surveyed it, and saw that it contained an exalted throne;

18 The appearance of which was like that of frost; while its circumference resembled the orb of the brilliant sun; and *there was* the voice of the cherubim.

19 From underneath this mighty throne rivers of flaming fire issued.

20 To look upon it was impossible.

21 One great in esteem sat upon it:

22 Whose robe was brighter than the sun, and whiter than snow.

23 No malakh was capable of penetrating to view the face of Him, the Esteemed and the Effulgent; nor could any mortal behold Him. A fire was flaming around Him.

24 A fire also of great extent continued to rise up before Him; so that no one of the one's who surrounded Him was capable of approaching Him, among the myriads of myriads[1] who were before Him. To Him set-apart consultation was needless. Yet did not the sanctified, who were near Him, depart far from Him either by night or by

---

[1] Ten thousand times ten thousand that is ten billion angels.

Seferim Khanok

day; nor were they removed from Him. I also was so far advanced, with a veil on my face, and trembling. Then the Master with his *own* mouth called me, saying, approach here, Khanok, at my set-apart word.

25 And He raised me up, making me draw near even to the entrance. My eye was directed to the ground.

Chapter 15

1 Then addressing me, He spoke and said, Hear, neither be afraid, O tsadik Khanok, you scribe of right-ruling: approach here, and hear my voice. Go, say to the Watchers of shamayim, who have sent you to petition[1] for them, You ought to petition[2] for men, and not men for you.

2 Why have you forsaken the lofty and set-apart shamayim, which endures for ever, and have lain with women; have defiled yourselves with the daughters of men; have taken to yourselves wives; have acted like the sons of the eretz, and have begotten giants?[3]

3 You being spiritual, set-apart, and possessing a life which is eternal, have polluted yourselves with women; have begotten in carnal blood; have lusted in the blood of men; and have done as those *who are* flesh and blood do.

4 These however die and perish.[4]

5 Therefore have I given to them wives, that they might cohabit with them; that sons might be born of them; and that this might be established upon eretz.

6 But you from the beginning were made spiritual, possessing a life which is eternal, and not subject to death forever.[1]

---

[1] Petition here means to appeal for them or take their cause to heaven.
[2] It is the angels job to carry our petitions up and not vice versa.
[3] Many bones of big giants are found in the middle-eastern and Asian regions some men who were 32 feet tall and even greater than these.
[4] Men do not have eternal life nor eternal souls unless they have the obedience to the Torah of YHWH, that has all the contracts.

7 Therefore I made no wives for you, because, being spiritual, your dwelling is in shamayim.[2]

8 Now the giants, who have been born of ruakh and of flesh, shall be called upon eretz unclean ruakhot, and on eretz shall be their habitation.[3] Unclean ruakhot shall proceed from their flesh, because they were created from above; from the set-apart Watchers was their beginning and primary foundation. Unclean ruakhot shall they be upon eretz, and the ruakh of the wicked shall they be called. The habitation of the ruakhot of shamayim shall be in shamayim; but upon eretz shall be the habitation of terrestrial ruakhot, who are born on eretz.

9 The ruakhot of the giants *shall be like* clouds, which shall oppress, corrupt, fall, content, and bruise upon eretz.[4]

10 They shall cause lamentation. No food shall they eat;[5] and they shall be thirsty;[6] they shall be concealed, and shall not rise up against the sons of men, and against women; for they come forth during the days of slaughter and destruction.

Chapter 16
1 And as to the death of the giants, wherever their ruakhot depart from their bodies, let their flesh, that which is perishable, be destroyed without judgment. Thus shall they perish, until the day of the great consummation of the great world. A destruction shall take place of the Watchers and the impious.

---

[1] Hence why these angels will be punished forever and forever as they cannot die. The lake of fire was built for rebellious angels but when men are thrown into it their souls become ash so to speak non-existant and or terminated.

[2] Angels mostly are masculine. Shaitan is asexual.

[3] Upon their death these giants were turned into demons. This is the second source for demons. While the first woman Lilith was also turned into a demoness and all her offspring. See AF Hebraic Study Bible footnote Isa 34:14.

[4] The Greek word for "clouds" nephelas could be read Nephilim.

[5] They are not designed like humans.

[6] These have been banished in dry and desert type locations where they feel thirst but cannot have any drink of water.

Seferim Khanok

2 And now to the Watchers, who have sent you to petition for them, who in the beginning were in shamayim,

3 *Say*, in shamayim have you been; secret things, however, have not been manifested to you; yet have you known a reprobate mystery.

4 And this you have related to women in the hardness of your heart, and by that mystery have women and mankind multiplied evils upon the eretz.

5 Say to them, Never therefore shall you obtain shalom.

Chapter 17
1 They raised me up into a certain place, where there was the appearance of a burning fire; and when they pleased they assumed the likeness of men.

2 They carried me to a lofty spot, to a mountain, the top of which reach to shamayim.

3 And I beheld the receptacles of light and of thunder at the extremities of the place, where it was deepest. There was a bow of fire, and arrows in their quiver, a sword of fire, and every species of lightning.

4 Then they elevated me to the mayim of life, and to a fire in the west, which received all the setting of the sun. I came to a river of fire, which flowed like mayim, and emptied itself into the great sea westwards.

5 I saw every large river, until I arrived at the great darkness. I went to where all of flesh migrate; and I beheld the mountains of the gloom which constitutes winter, and the place from which issues the mayim in every abyss.

6 I saw also the mouths of all the rivers in the world, and the mouths of the deep.

Chapter 18
1I then surveyed the receptacles of all the winds, perceiving that they contributed to adorn the whole creation, and *to preserve* the foundation of the eretz.

Seferim Khanok

2 I surveyed the stone *which supports* the corners of the eretz.

3 I also beheld the four winds, which bear up the eretz, and the firmament of shamayim.

4 And I beheld the winds occupying the exalted sky.

5 Arising in the midst of shamayim and of eretz, and constituting the pillars of shamayim.

6 I saw the winds which turn the sky, which cause the orb of the sun and of all the stars to set; and over the eretz I saw the winds which support the clouds.

7 I saw the path of the malakhim.

8 I perceived at the extremity of the eretz the firmament of shamayim above it. Then I passed on towards the south;

9 Where burnt, both by day and night, six mountains formed of esteemed stones; three towards the east, and three towards the south.

10 Those which were towards the east were of a variegated stone; one of which was of margarite, and another of antimony. Those towards the south were of a red stone. The middle one reached to shamayim like the throne of Elohim; *a throne composed* of alabaster, the top of which was of sapphire. I saw, too, a blazing fire hanging over all the mountains.

11 And there I saw a place on the other side of an extended territory, where waters were collected.

12 I likewise beheld terrestrial fountains, deep in the fiery columns of shamayim.

13 And in the columns of shamayim I beheld fires, which descended without number, but neither on high, nor into the deep. Over these fountains also I perceived a place which had neither the firmament of shamayim above it, nor

Seferim Khanok

the solid ground underneath it; neither was there mayim above it; nor anything on wing; but the spot was desolate.

14 And there I beheld seven stars, like great blazing mountains, and like ruakhot entreating me.

15 Then the malakh said, this place, until the consummation of shamayim and eretz, will be the prison of the stars, and the host of shamayim.

16 The stars which roll over fire are those which transgressed the commandment of Elohim before their time arrived; for they came not in their proper season. Therefore was He offended with them, and bound them, until the period of the consummation of their crimes in the secret year.

Chapter 19

1 Then Uri'el said, here the malakhim, who cohabited with women, appointed their leaders;

2 And assuming different forms[1] made men profane, and caused them to err; so that they sacrificed to devils as to mighty ones. For in the great day *there shall be* a judgment, with which they shall be judged, until they are consumed; and their wives also shall be *judged,* who led astray the malakhim of shamayim that they might greet them.[2]

3 And I, Khanok, I alone saw the likeness of the end of all things. Nor did any human being see it, as I saw it.[3]

---

[1] Angels went in different forms to deceive mankind into making them think that the stones and statues they started to make to worship were the creators of the earth.

[2] The women knew that these beings were not of the earth but above but in spite of that because they perceived to have marriage with these beings into receiving power and magical authority.

[3] Khanok was shown the end of days and the world to come the millennium kingdom. Note Khanok was not a white Caucasian as portrayed. He was the line of Ahdham, what is mud when you mix it? It is very dark brown to black hew and that was the colour of Ahdham. Qayin went and settled in the land of Nod/Nok in West Africa and there

Seferim Khanok

Chapter 20
1 These are the names of the malakhim who watch.

2 Uri'el, one of the set-apart malakhim, who *presides* over clamor and terror.

3 Raphael, one of the set-apart malakhim, who *presides* over the ruakhot of men.

4 Raguel, one of the set-apart malakhim, who inflicts punishment on the world and the luminaries.

5 Micha'el, one of the set-apart malakhim, who, *presiding* over human virtue, commands the nations.[1]

6 Sarakiel, one of the set-apart malakhim, who *presides* over the ruakhot of the children of men that transgress.

7 Gabri'el, one of the set-apart malakhim, who *presides* over Ikisat,[2] over paradise, and over the cherubim.

Chapter 21
1 Then I made a circuit to a place in which nothing was completed.

2 And there I beheld neither the tremendous workmanship of an exalted shamayim, nor of an established eretz, but a desolate spot, prepared, and terrific.

3 There, too, I beheld seven stars of shamayim bound in it together, like great mountains, and like a blazing fire. I exclaimed, for what species of crime have they been bound, and why have they been removed to this place?[3] Then Uri'el, one of the set-apart malakhim who was with me, and who conducted me, answered: Khanok, Why do you ask; why *do you* reason with yourself, and anxiously inquire? These are those of the stars which have transgressed the commandment of the most high Elohim;

---

the majority of the folks that followed including Khanok were of black colour.
[1] He also looks after Y'sra'el.
[2] Serpents.
[3] These are Angels that were bound in prison.

Seferim Khanok

and are here bound, until the infinite number of the days of their crimes be completed.

4 From there I afterwards passed on to another terrific place;

5 Where I beheld the operation of a great fire blazing and glittering, in the midst of which there was a division. Columns of fire struggled together to the end of the abyss, and deep was their descent. But neither its measurement nor magnitude was I able to discover; neither could I perceive its origin. Then I exclaimed, how terrible is this place, and how difficult to explore!

6 Uri'el, one of the set-apart malakhim who was with me, answered and said: Khanok, why are you alarmed and amazed at this terrific place, at the sight of this *place of suffering?* This, he said, is the prison of the malakhim; and here they are kept for ever.

Chapter 22

1 From there I proceeded to another spot, where I saw on the west a great and lofty mountain, a strong rock, and four delightful places.

2 Internally it was deep, capacious, and very smooth; as smooth as if it had been rolled over: it was both deep and dark to behold.

3 Then Raphael, one of the set-apart malakhim who were with me, answered and said, These are the delightful places where the ruakhot, the souls of the dead, will be collected; for them were they formed; and here will be collected all the souls of the sons of men.

4 These places, in which they dwell, shall they occupy until the Day of Judgment and until their appointed period.[1]

---

[1] Wicked souls bound in chambers until the great judgment and the right ruling souls in paradise, the conceptual view is from heaven while they are not in heaven.

Seferim Khanok

5 Their appointed period will be long, even until the great judgment. And I saw the ruakhot of the sons of men who were dead; and their voices reached to shamayim, while they were accusing.

6 Then I inquired of Raphael, a malakh who was with me, and said, whose ruakh is that, the voice of which reaches *to shamayim*, and accuses?

7 He answered, saying, this is the ruakh of Hebel who was slain by Qayin his brother; and who will accuse that brother, until his seed be destroyed from the face of the eretz;

8 Until his seed perish from the seed of the human race.

9 At that time therefore I inquired respecting him, and respecting the general judgment, saying, why is one separated from another? He answered, three *separations* have been made between the ruakhot of the dead, and thus have the ruakhot of the tsadik been separated.[1]

10 Namely, *by* a chasm, *by* mayim, and *by* light[2] above it.

11 And in the same way likewise are transgressors separated when they die, and are buried in the eretz; judgment not overtaking them in their lifetime.

12 Here their souls are separated. Moreover, abundant is their suffering until the time of the great judgment, the castigation, and the torment of those who eternally curse whose souls are punished and bound there for ever.[3]

13 And thus has it been from the beginning of the world. Thus has there existed a separation between the souls of those who utter complaints, and of those who watch for

---

[1] The right-ruling live in paradise which is a section of She'ol setup to accommodate the right-ruling dead. There is water separating them and light. The sinners cannot cross over to the other side.
[2] Light and water separate the sinners and the right rulers in She'ol.
[3] Bound in chambers of a prison like structure with some cells being open and others closes darkness accompanying them. They are punished by demons.

their destruction, to destroy[1] them in the day of transgressors.

14 A receptacle of this sort has been formed for the souls of unruly men, and of transgressors; of those who have completed crime, and associated with the impious, which they resemble. Their souls shall not be annihilated in the Day of Judgment neither shall they arise from this place. Then I magnified Elohim,

15 And said, Benevolent is my Master, YHWH of esteem and of right-ruling, who reigns over all for ever and for ever.

Chapter 23
1 From there I went to another place, towards the west, unto the extremities of the eretz.[2]

2 Where I beheld a fire blazing and running along without cessation, which intermitted its course neither by day nor by night; but continued always the same.

3 I inquired, saying, what is this, which never ceases?

4 Then Raguel one of the set-apart malakhim who were with me, answered,

5 And said, this blazing fire, which you behold running towards the west, is *that of* all the luminaries of shamayim.

Chapter 24
1 I went from there to another place, and saw a mountain of fire flashing both by day and night. I proceeded towards it; and perceived seven splendid mountains,[3] which were all different from each other.

---

[1] These will be destroyed in the final lake of fire judgment. John 3:16.
[2] This west is not as we perceive it but the extremities of the African regions such as Muritania.
[3] In the region of Saudi Arabia where the set-apart Mountain is where the Torah was given called Horeb or Mount Sinai. This mountain is not in Egypt.

Seferim Khanok

2 Their stones were brilliant and beautiful; all were brilliant and splendid to behold; and beautiful was their surface. Three *mountains* were towards the east, and strengthened by being placed one upon another; and three were towards the south, strengthened in a similar manner. There were likewise deep valleys, which did not approach each other. And the seventh mountain was in the midst of them. In length they all resembled the seat of a throne, and fragrant etzim surrounded them.

3 Among these there was an etz of an unceasing smell; nor of those which were in Ayden was there one of all the fragrant etzim which smelt like this. Its leaf, its flower, and its bark never withered, and its fruit was beautiful.

4 Its fruit resembled the cluster of the palm. I exclaimed, Behold! This etz is good in aspect, pleasing in its leaf, and the sight of its fruit is delightful to the eye. Then Micha'el, one of the set-apart and esteemed malakhim who were with me, and *one* who presided over them, answered,

5 And said: Khanok, why do you inquire respecting the fragrant of this etz?

6 *Why* are you inquisitive to know it?

7 Then I, Khanok, replied to him, and said, concerning everything I am desirous of instruction, but particularly concerning this etz.

8 He answered me, saying, that mountain which you behold, the extent of whose head resembles the seat of the Master, will be the seat on which shall sit the set-apart and great Master of esteem, the everlasting King, when he shall come and descend to visit the eretz with goodness.

9 And that etz of an agreeable smell, not one of carnal *fragrant*, there shall be no power to touch, until the period of the great judgment. When all shall be punished and consumed for ever, this shall be bestowed on the tsadik and humble. The fruit of the *etz* shall be given to the elect.

Seferim Khanok

For towards the north[1] life shall be planted in the set-apart place, towards the habitation of the everlasting King.

10 Then shall they greatly rejoice and exult in the Set-apart One. The sweet fragrant shall enter into their bones; and they shall live a long life on the eretz as your forefathers have lived; neither in their days shall sorrow, distress, trouble, and punishment afflict them.

11 And I magnified YHWH of esteem, the everlasting King, because He has prepared *this etz* for the kedushim, formed it, and declared that He would give it to them.

Chapter 25

1 From there I proceeded to the middle of the eretz, and beheld a happy and fertile spot, which contained branches continually sprouting from the etzim which were planted in it. There I saw a set-apart mountain, and underneath it mayim on the eastern side, which flowed towards the south. I saw also on the east another mountain as high as that; and between them there were deep, but not wide valleys.

2 Water ran towards the mountain to the west of this; and underneath there was likewise another mountain.

3 There was a valley, but not a wide one, below it; and in the midst of them were other deep and dry valleys towards the extremity of the three. All these valleys, which were deep, but not side, consisted of a strong rock, with an etz which was planted in them. And I wondered at the rock and at the valleys, being extremely surprised.

Chapter 26

1 Then I said, what means this increased land, all these lofty etzim, and the accursed valley between them?

2 Then Uri'el, one of the set-apart malakhim who was with me, replied, this valley is the accursed of the accursed for ever. Here shall be collected all who utter with their mouths

---

[1] The vantage point of Southern Africa so North would be Y'sra'el and also the North is the place of the 3rd heavens where YHWH lives.

Seferim Khanok

unbecoming language against Elohim, and speak harsh things of His esteem.[1] Here shall they be collected. Here shall be their territory.

3 In the latter days an example of judgment shall be made of them in right-ruling before the kedushim; while those who have received mercy shall for ever, all their days, say benevolent is Elohim, the everlasting King.

4 And at the period of judgment shall they exalt Him for his mercy, as He has distributed it to them. Then I exalted Elohim, addressing myself to Him, and making mention, as was meet, of His greatness.

Chapter 27
1 From there I proceeded towards the east to the middle of the mountain in the desert, the level surface only of which I perceived.

2 It was full of etzim of the seed alluded to; and mayim leaped down upon it.

3 There appeared a cataract composed as of many cataracts both towards the west and towards the east. Upon one side were etzim; upon the other mayim and dew.

Chapter 28
1 Then I went to another place from the desert; towards the east of that mountain *which* I had approached.

2 There I beheld choice etzim, particularly, *those which produce* the sweet-smelling opiate, frankincense and myrrh; and etzim unlike to each other.

3 And over it, above them, was the elevation of the eastern mountain at no great distance.

Chapter 29
1 I likewise saw another place with valleys of mayim which never wasted,

---

[1] This place is designated for the atheists and those who hate Elohim of Y'sra'el.

Seferim Khanok

2 *Where* I perceived a goodly etz, which in smell resembled Zasakinon.

3 And towards the sides of these valleys I perceived cinnamon of a sweet fragrant. Over them I advanced towards the east.

Chapter 30
1 Then I beheld another mountain containing etzim, from which mayim flowed like Nectar, Its name was Styrax, and Kalboneba. And upon this mountain I beheld another mountain, upon which were etzim of Aloe.

2 These etzim were full, like almond etzim, and strong; and when they produced fruit, it was superior to all redolence.

Chapter 31
1 After these things, surveying the entrances of the north, above the mountains, I perceived seven mountains replete with pure nard, fragrance etzim of cinnamon and papyrus.

2 From there I passed on above the summits of those mountains to some distance eastwards, and went over the Eritrean Sea.[1] And when I was advanced far beyond it, I passed along above the malakh Zateel, and arrived at the garden of right-ruling. In this garden I beheld, among other etzim, some which were numerous and large, and which flourished there.

3 Their fragrance was agreeable and powerful, and their appearance both varied and elegant. The etz of knowledge also was there, of which if any one eats, he becomes endowed with great wisdom.

4 It was like a species of the tamarind etz, bearing fruit which resembled grapes extremely fine; and its fragrance extended to a considerable distance. I exclaimed, how beautiful is this etz, and how delightful is its appearance!

5 Then set-apart Raphael, a malakh who was with me, answered and said, this is the etz of knowledge, of which

---

[1] Passing over modern Eritrea in African crossing the Red Sea.

your ancient father and your aged mother ate, who were before you; and who, obtaining knowledge, their eyes being opened, and knowing themselves to be naked, were expelled from the garden.

Chapter 32
1 From there I went on towards the extremities of the eretz; where I saw large beasts different from each other, and birds various in their countenances and forms, as well as with notes of different sounds.

2 To the east of these beasts I perceived the extremities of the eretz, where shamayim ceased. The gates of shamayim stood open, and I beheld the celestial stars come forth. I numbered them as they proceeded out of the gate, and wrote them all down, as they came out one by one according to their number. *I wrote down* their names altogether, their times and their seasons, as the malakh Uri'el, who was with me, pointed them out to me.

3 He showed them all to me, and wrote down *an account of* them.

4 He also wrote down for me their names, their regulations, and their operations.

Chapter 33
1 From there I advanced on towards the north, to the extremities of the eretz.

2 And there I saw a great and esteemed wonder at the extremities of the whole eretz.

3 I saw there heavenly gates opening into shamayim; three of them distinctly separated. The northern winds proceeded from them, blowing cold, hail, frost, snow, dew, and rain.

4 From one of the gates they blew mildly; but when they blew from the two *other gates*, it was with violence and force. They blew over the eretz strongly.

Chapter 34

Seferim Khanok

1 From there I went to the extremities of the world westwards;[1]

2 Where I perceived three gates open, as I had seen in the north; the gates and passages through them being of equal magnitude.

Chapter 35
1 Then I proceeded to the extremities of the eretz southwards;[2] where I saw three gates open to the south, from which issued dew, rain, and wind.

2 From there I went to the extremities of shamayim eastwards; where I saw three heavenly gates open to the east, which had smaller gates within them. Through each of these small gates the stars of shamayim passed on, and proceeded towards the west by a path which was seen by them, and that at every period *of their appearance.*

3 When I beheld *them,* I magnified; every time *in which they appeared,* I magnified YHWH of esteem, who had made those great and splendid signs, that they might display the magnificence of this works to malakhim and to the souls of men; and that these might glorify all his works and operations; might see the effect of his power; might glorify the great labour of his hands; and benevolent is he for ever.

Chapter 36 does not exist

Chapter 37
1 The vision which he saw, the second vision of wisdom, which Khanok saw, the son of Yared, the son of Mahalale'el, the son of Qaynan, the son of Enosh, the son of Sheth, the son of Ahdahm. This is the commencement of the word of wisdom, which I received to declare and tell to those who dwell upon eretz. Hear from the beginning, and understand to the end, the set-apart things which I utter in the presence of YHWH of ruakhot. Those who were before *us* thought it good to speak;

---

[1] He was on the edge of the African continent.
[2] Deep down into South Africa.

2 And let not us, who come after, obstruct the beginning of wisdom. Until the present period never has there been given before YHWH of ruakhot that which I have received, wisdom according the capacity of my intellect, and according to the pleasure of YHWH of ruakhot; that which I have received from him, a portion of life eternal.

3 And I obtained three parables, which I declared to the inhabitants of the world.

Chapter 38
1 Parable the first. When the congregation of the tsadik shall be manifested; and transgressors be judged for their crimes, and be troubled in the sight of the world;

2 When right-ruling shall be manifested in the presence of the tsadik themselves, who will be elected for their *good Torah* works *duly* weighed by YHWH of ruakhot; and when the light of the tsadik and the elect, who dwell on eretz, shall be manifested; where will the habitation of transgressors be? And where the place of rest for those who have rejected the Master of ruakhot? It would have been better for them, had they never been born.

3 When, too, the secrets of The Tsadik shall be revealed, then shall transgressors be judged; and impious men shall be afflicted in the presence of the tsadik and the elect.

4 From that period those who possess the eretz shall cease to be powerful and exalted. Neither shall they be capable of beholding the countenances of the Set-Apart; for the light of the countenances of the Set-Apart, the Tsadik, and the elect, has been seen by the Master of ruakhot.

5 Yet shall not the mighty kings of that period be destroyed; but be delivered into the hands of the Tsadik and the Set-Apart.

6 Nor thenceforwards shall any obtain commiseration from the Master of ruakhot, because their lives *in this world* will have been completed.

Seferim Khanok

Chapter 39

1 In those days shall the elect and set-apart race descend from the upper shamayim, and their seed shall then be with the sons of men. Khanok received books of indignation and wrath, and books of hurry and agitation.

2 Never shall they obtain mercy, says the Master of ruakhot.

3 A cloud then snatched me up, and the wind raised me above the surface of the eretz, placing me at the extremity of the shamayim.

4 There I saw another vision; I *saw* the habitations and resting places of the kedushim. There my eyes beheld their habitations with the malakhim, and their resting places with the set-apart ones. They were entreating, supplicating, and praying for the sons of men; while right-ruling like mayim flowed before them, and mercy like dew *was scattered* over the eretz. And thus *shall it be* with them for ever and for ever.

5 At that time my eyes beheld the dwelling of the elect, of truth, faith, and right-ruling.

6 Countless shall be the number of the set-apart and the elect, in the presence of Elohim for ever and forever.

7 Their residence I beheld under the wings of the Master of ruakhot. All the set-apart and the elect sung before him, in appearance like a blaze of fire; their mouths being full of increases, and their lips esteeming the name of YHWH of ruakhot. And right-ruling incessantly *dwelt* before him.

8 There was I desirous of remaining, and my soul longed for that habitation. There was my antecedent inheritance; for thus had I prevailed before YHWH of ruakhot.

9 At that time I esteemed and extolled the name of YHWH of ruakhot with magnifying and with praise; for he has established it with magnifying and with praise, according to his own good pleasure.

Seferim Khanok

10 That place long did my eyes contemplate. I magnified and said, magnified be he, Benevolent from the beginning for ever. In the beginning, before the world was created, and without end is his knowledge.

11 What is this world? Of every existing generation those shall say benevolent are you who do not *spiritually* sleep but stand before your esteem, magnifying, glorifying, exalting you, and saying, The set-apart, set-apart, YHWH of ruakhot, fills the whole world of ruakhot.

12 There my eyes beheld all who, without sleeping, stand before him and exalt him, saying, Benevolent be you, and Benevolent be the name of YHWH for ever and for ever. Then my countenance became changed, until I was incapable of seeing.

Chapter 40
1 After this I beheld thousands of thousands, and myriads of myriads, and an infinite number of people, standing before YHWH of ruakhot.

2 On the four wings likewise of the Master of ruakhot, on the four sides, I perceived others, besides those who were standing *before him.* Their names, too, I know; because the malakh, who proceeded with me, declared them to me, discovering to me every secret thing.

3 Then I heard the voices of those upon the four sides magnifying YHWH of esteem.

4 The first voice magnified YHWH of ruakhot for ever and for ever.

5 The second voice I heard magnifying the Elect One, and the elect who suffer on account of the Master of ruakhot.

6 The third voice I heard petitioning and praying for those who dwell upon eretz, and supplicate the name of YHWH of ruakhot.

Seferim Khanok

7 The fourth voice I heard expelling the impious devils, and prohibiting them from entering into the presence of YHWH of ruakhot, to accuse against the inhabitants of the eretz.

8 After this I besought the malakh of shalom, who proceeded with me, to explain all that was concealed. I said to him, who are those *whom* I have seen on the four sides, and whose words I have heard and written down? He replied, the first is the merciful, the patient, the set-apart Micha'el.

9 The second is he who *presides* over every suffering and every affliction of the sons of men, the set-apart Raphael. The third, who *presides* over all that is powerful, is Gabri'el. And the fourth, who *presides* over repentance, and the hope of those who will inherit eternal life, is Phanuel. These are the four malakhim of the most high Elohim, and their four voices, which at that time I heard.

Chapter 41
1 After this I beheld the secrets of the shamayim and of paradise, according to its divisions; and of human action, as they weight it there in balances. I saw the habitations of the elect, and the habitations of the set-apart. And there my eyes beheld all the transgressors, who denied YHWH of esteem, and whom they were expelling from there, and dragging away, as they stood *there*; no punishment proceeding against them from the Master of ruakhot.

2 There, too, my eyes beheld the secrets of the lightning and the thunder; and the secrets of the winds, how they are distributed as they blow over the eretz: the secrets of the winds, of the dew, and of the clouds. There I perceived the place from which they issued forth, and became saturated with the dust of the eretz.

3 There I saw the wooden receptacles out of which the winds became separated, the receptacle of hail, the receptacle of snow, the receptacle of the clouds, and the cloud itself, *which* continued over the eretz before *the creation of* the world.

4 I beheld also the receptacles of the moon, from where they came, whither they proceeded, their esteemed return, and how one became more splendid than another. I *marked* their rich progress, their unchangeable progress, their disunited and undiminished progress; their observance of a mutual fidelity by a stable oath; their proceeding forth before the sun, and their adherence to the path *allotted* them, in obedience to the command of the Master of ruakhot. Potent is his name for ever and for ever.

5 After this *I perceived, that* the path both concealed and manifest of the moon, as well as the progress of its path, was there completed by day and by night; while each, one with another, looked towards the Master of ruakhot, magnifying and praising without cessation, since praise to them is rest; for in the splendid sun there is a frequent conversion to magnifying and to malediction.

6 The course of the moon's path to the tsadik is light, but to transgressors it is darkness; in the name of YHWH of ruakhot, who created *a division* between light and darkness, and, separating the ruakhot of men, strengthened the ruakhot of the tsadik in the name of his own right-ruling.

7 Nor does the malakh prevent *this*, neither is he endowed with the power of preventing it; for the Judge beholds them all, and judges them all in his own presence.

Chapter 42
1 Wisdom found not a place *on eretz* where she could inhabit; her dwelling therefore is in shamayim.

2 Wisdom went forth to dwell among the sons of men, but she obtained not a habitation. Wisdom returned to her place, and seated herself in the midst of the malakhim. But iniquity went forth after her return, who unwillingly found *a habitation,* and resided among them, as rain in the desert, and as a dew in a thirsty land.

Chapter 43
1 I beheld another splendor and the stars of shamayim. I observed that he called them all by their respective names,

Seferim Khanok

and that they heard. In a tsadik balance I saw that he weighed out with their light the amplitude of their places, and the day of their appearance, and their conversion. Splendor produced splendor; and their conversion *was* into the number of the malakhim, and of the faithful.

2 Then I inquired of the malakh, who proceeded with me, and explained to me secret things, what *their names* were. He answered. A similitude of those has the Master of ruakhot shown you. They are names of the tsadik who dwell upon eretz, and who believe in the name of YHWH of ruakhot for ever and for ever.

Chapter 44
1 Another thing also I saw respecting splendor; that it rises out of the stars, and becomes splendor; being incapable of forsaking them.

Chapter 45
1 Parable the second, respecting these who deny the name of the habitation of the set-apart ones, and of the Master of ruakhot.

2 Shamayim they shall not ascend, nor shall they come on the eretz. This shall be the portion of transgressors, who deny the name of YHWH of ruakhot, and who are thus reserved for the day of punishment and of affliction.

3 In that day shall the Elect One sit upon a throne of esteem; and shall choose their conditions and countless habitations, while their ruakhot within them shall be strengthened, when they behold my Elect One, for those who have fled for protection to my set-apart and esteemed name.

4 In that day I will cause my Elect One to dwell in the midst of them; will change *the face of* shamayim; will increase it, and illuminate it for ever.

5 I will also change *the face of* the eretz, will increase it; and cause those whom I have elected to dwell upon it. But those who have committed transgression and iniquity shall not inhabit it, for I have marked their proceedings. My tsadik ones will I satisfy with shalom, placing them before me; but the condemnation of transgressors shall draw near, that I may destroy them from the face of the eretz.

Chapter 46

1 There I beheld the Ancient of days, whose head was like white wool, and with him another, whose countenance resembled that of man. His countenance was full of grace, like *that of* one of the set-apart malakhim. Then I inquired of one of the malakhim, who went with me, and who showed me every secret thing, concerning this Son of man; who he was; whence he was and why he accompanied the Ancient of days.

2 He answered and said to me, This is the Son of man, to whom right-ruling belongs; with whom right-ruling has dwelt; and who will reveal all the treasures of that which is concealed: for the Master of ruakhot has chosen him; and his portion has surpassed all before the Master of ruakhot in everlasting uprightness.

3 This Son of man, whom you behold, shall raise up kings and the mighty from their dwelling places, and the powerful from their thrones; shall loosen the bridles of the powerful, and break in pieces the teeth of transgressors.

4 He shall hurl kings from their thrones and their dominions; because they will not exalt and praise him, nor humble themselves *before him*, by whom their kingdoms were granted to them. The countenance likewise of the mighty shall He cast down, filling them with confusion. Darkness shall be their habitation, and worms shall be their bed; nor from *that* their bed shall they hope to be again raised, because they exalted not the name of YHWH of ruakhot.

5 They shall condemn the stars of shamayim, shall lift up their hands against the Most High, shall tread upon and inhabit the eretz, exhibiting all their acts of iniquity, even their works of iniquity. Their strength shall be in their riches, and their faith in the elohim whom they have formed with their own hands. They shall deny the name of the

Seferim Khanok

Master of ruakhot, and shall expel him from the temples, in which they assemble;

6 And *with him* the faithful *will be driven out*, who suffer in the name of YHWH of ruakhot.

Chapter 47
1 In that day the petition of the set-apart and the tsadik, and the blood of the tsadik, shall ascend from the eretz into the presence of the Master of ruakhot.

2 In that day shall the set-apart ones assemble, who dwell above the shamayim, and with united voice petition, supplicate, praise, laud, and benevolent is the name of YHWH of ruakhot, on account of the blood of the tsadik which has been shed; that the petition of the tsadik may not be intermitted before the Master of ruakhot; that for them he would execute judgment; and that his patience may not endure for ever.

3 At that time I beheld the Ancient of days, while he sat upon the throne of his esteem, *while* the book of the living[1] was opened in his presence, and *while* all the powers which were above the shamayim stood around and before him.

4 Then were the hearts of the kedushim full of joy, because the consummation of right-ruling was arrived, the supplication of the kedushim heard, and the blood of the tsadik appreciated by the Master of ruakhot.

Chapter 48
1 In that place I beheld a fountain of right-ruling, which never failed, encircled by many springs of wisdom. Of these all the thirsty drank, and were filled with wisdom, having their habitation with the tsadik, the elect, and the set-apart.

---

[1] There are several books in heaven keeping record of people upon the earth.

Seferim Khanok

2 In that hour was this Son of man invoked before the Master of ruakhot, and his name in the presence of the Ancient of days.

3 Before the sun and the signs were created, before the stars of shamayim were formed, his name was invoked in the presence of the Master of ruakhot. A support shall he be for the tsadik and the set-apart to lean upon, without falling; and he shall be the light of nations.

4 He shall be the hope of those whose hearts are troubled. All, who dwell on eretz, shall fall down and worship before him; shall say Benevolent is he and glorify him, and sing praises to the name of YHWH of ruakhot.

5 Therefore the Elect and the Concealed One existed in his presence, before the world was created, and for ever.

6 In his presence *he existed,* and has revealed to the kedushim and to the tsadik the wisdom of the Master of ruakhot; for he has preserved the lot of the tsadik, because they have hated and rejected this world of iniquity, and have detested all its works and ways, in the name of YHWH of ruakhot.

7 For in his name shall they be preserved; and his will shall be their life. In those days shall the kings of the eretz and the mighty men, who have gained the world by their achievements, become humble in countenance.

8 For in the day of their anxiety and trouble their souls shall not be saved; and *they shall be* in subjection to those whom I have chosen.

9 I will cast them like hay into the fire, and like lead into the mayim. Thus shall they burn in the presence of the tsadik, and sink in the presence of the set-apart; nor shall a tenth part of them be found.

10 But in the day of their trouble, the world shall obtain tranquility.

Seferim Khanok

11 In his presence shall they fall, and not be raised up again; nor shall there be any one to take them out of his hands, and to lift them up: for they have denied YHWH of ruakhot, and His Anointed. The name of YHWH of ruakhot shall be magnified.

Chapter 48A[1]
1 Wisdom is poured forth like mayim, and esteem fails not before him for ever and ever; for potent is he in all the secrets of right-ruling.

2 But iniquity passes away like a shadow, and possesses not a fixed station: for the Elect One stands before the Master of ruakhot; and his esteem is for ever and ever; and his power from generation to generation.

3 With him dwells the Ruakh of intellectual wisdom, the Ruakh of instruction and of power,[2] and the ruakh of those who sleep in right-ruling; he shall judge secret things.

4 Nor shall any be able to utter a single word before him; for the Elect One is in the presence of the Master of Ruakhot, according to his own pleasure.

Chapter 49
1 In those days the kedushim and the chosen shall undergo a change. The light of day shall rest upon them; and the splendor and esteem of the kedushim shall be changed.

2 In the day of trouble evil shall be heaped up upon transgressors; but the tsadik shall triumph in the name of YHWH of ruakhot.

3 Others shall be made to see, that they must repent, and forsake the works of their hands; and that esteem awaits them not in the presence of the Master of ruakhot; yet that by his name they may be saved. YHWH of ruakhot will have compassion on them; for great is his mercy; and right-ruling is in his judgment, and in the presence of his

---

[1] Because two chapters are numbered 48 therefore one has to be called 48A here.
[2] The Holy Spirit.

esteem; nor in his judgment shall iniquity stand. He who repents not before him shall perish.

4 Henceforward I will not have mercy on them, says the Master of ruakhot.

Chapter 50
1 In those days shall the eretz deliver up from her womb, and hell deliver up from hers, that which it has received; and destruction shall restore that which it owes.

2 He shall select the tsadik and set-apart from among them; for the day of their salvation has approached.

3 And in those days shall the Elect One sit upon his throne, while every secret of intellectual wisdom shall proceed from his mouth, for YHWH of ruakhot has gifted and esteemed him.

4 In those days the mountains shall skip like rams, and the hills shall leap like young sheep satiated with milk; and all *the tsadik* shall become *like* malakhim in shamayim.

5 Their countenance shall be bright with joy; for in those days shall the Elect One be exalted. The eretz shall rejoice; the tsadik shall inhabit it, and the elect possess it.

Chapter 51
1 After that period, in the place where I had seen every secret sight, I was snatched up in a whirlwind, and carried off westwards.

2 There my eyes beheld the secrets of shamayim, and all which existed on eretz; a mountain of iron, a mountain of copper, a mountain of silver, a mountain of gold, a mountain of fluid metal, and a mountain of lead.

3 And I inquired of the malakh who went with me, saying, what are these things, which in secret I behold?

4 He said, All these things which you behold shall be for the dominion of the Messiah, that he may command, and be powerful upon eretz.

Seferim Khanok

5 And that malakh of shalom answered me, saying, wait but a short time, and you shall understand, and every secret thing shall be revealed to you, which the Master of ruakhot has decreed. Those mountains which you have seen, the mountain of iron, the mountain of copper, the mountain of silver, the mountain of gold, the mountain of fluid metal, and the mountain of lead, all these in the presence of the Elect One shall be like a honeycomb before the fire, and like mayim descending from above upon these mountains; and shall become debilitated before his feet.[1]

6 In those days men shall not be saved by gold and by silver.

7 Nor shall they have it in their power to secure themselves, and to fly.

8 There shall be neither iron for was, nor a coat of mail for the breast.

9 Copper shall be useless; useless also that which neither rusts nor consumes away; and lead shall not be coveted.

10 All these things shall be rejected, and perish from off the eretz, when the Elect One shall appear in the presence of the Master of ruakhot.

Chapter 52
1 There my eyes beheld a deep valley; and wide was its entrance.

2 All who dwell on land, on the sea, and in islands, shall bring to it gifts, presents, and offerings; yet that deep valley shall not be full. Their hands shall commit iniquity. Whatsoever they produce by labour the transgressors shall devour with crime. But they shall perish from the face of the Master of ruakhot, and from the face of his eretz. They shall stand up, and shall not fail for ever and ever.

---

[1] These mountains described kingdoms just like Daniel's vision in Dan 2.31-34.

Seferim Khanok

3 I beheld the malakhim of punishment, who were dwelling *there*, and preparing every instrument of HaStan.

4 Then I inquired of the malakh of shalom, who proceeded with me, for whom those instruments were preparing.

5 He said, These they are preparing for the kings and powerful ones of the eretz, that thus they may perish.

6 After which the tsadik and chosen house of his congregation shall appear, and thenceforward unchangeable in the name of the Master of ruakhot.

7 Nor shall those mountains exist in his presence as the eretz and the hills, as the fountains of mayim *exist*. And the tsadik shall be relieved from the vexation of transgressors.

Chapter 53

1 Then I looked and turned myself to another part of the eretz, where I beheld a deep valley burning with fire.

2 To this valley they brought monarchs and the mighty.

3 And there my eyes beheld the instruments which they were making, fetters of iron of great weight.

4 Then I inquired of the malakh of shalom, who proceeded with me, saying, For whom are these fetters and instruments prepared?

5 He replied, These are prepared for the host of Azazeel,[1] that they may be delivered over and adjudged to the lowest condemnation; and that their *rebellious* malakhim may be overwhelmed with hurled stones, as the Master of ruakhot has commanded.

6 Micha'el and Gabri'el, Raphael and Phanuel shall be strengthened in that day, and shall then cast them into a furnace of blazing fire, that the Master of ruakhot may be avenged of them for their crimes; because they became

---

[1] The rebellious angelic leader.

ministers of HaStan, and seduced those who dwell upon eretz.

7 In those days shall punishment go forth from the Master of ruakhot; and the receptacles of mayim which are above the shamayim shall be opened, and the fountains likewise, which are under the shamayim and under the eretz.

8 All the waters, which are in the shamayim and above them, shall be mixed together.

9 The mayim which is above shamayim shall be the agent male;

10 And the mayim which is under the eretz shall be the recipient female: and all shall be destroyed who dwell upon eretz, and who dwell under the extremities of shamayim.

11 By these means shall they understand the iniquity which they have committed on eretz: and by these means shall they perish.

Chapter 54

1 Afterwards the Ancient of days repented, and said, In vain have I destroyed all the inhabitants of the eretz.

2 And he swore by his great name, *saying*, Hence forwards I will not act thus towards all those who dwell upon eretz.

3 But I will place a sign in the shamayim;[1] and it shall be a faithful witness between me and them for ever, as long as the days of shamayim and eretz last upon the eretz.

4 Afterwards, according to this my decree, when I shall be disposed to seize them beforehand, by the instrumentality of malakhim, in the day of affliction and trouble, my wrath and my punishment shall remain upon them, my punishment and my wrath, says Elohim the Master of ruakhot.

---

[1] The Rainbow Gen 9:13.

Seferim Khanok

5 O you kings, O you mighty, who inhabit the world you shall behold my Elect One, sitting upon the throne of my esteem. And he shall judge Azazeel, all his associates, and all his hosts, in the name of the Master of ruakhot.

6 There likewise I beheld hosts of malakhim who were moving in punishment, confined in a network of iron and brass. Then I inquired of the malakh of shalom, who proceeded with me, To whom those under confinement were going.

7 He said, To each of their elect and their beloved, that they may be cast into the fountains and deep recesses of the valley.

8 And that valley shall be filled with their elect and beloved; the days of whose life shall be consumed, but the days of their error shall be innumerable.

9 Then shall princes combine together, and conspire. The chiefs of the east, among the Parthians and Medes, shall remove kings, in whom a ruakh of perturbation shall enter. They shall hurl them from their thrones, springing as lions from their dens, and like famished wolves into the midst of the flock.

10 They shall go up, and tread upon the land of their elect. The land of their elect shall be before them. The threshing-floor, the path, and the city of my tsadik *people* shall impede *the progress of* their horses. They shall rise up to destroy each other; their right hand shall be strengthened; nor shall a man acknowledge his friend or his brother;

11 Nor the son his father and his mother; until the number of the dead bodies shall be *completed*, by their death and punishment. Neither shall this take place without cause.

12 In those days shall the mouth of hell be opened, into which they shall be immerged; hell shall destroy and swallow up transgressors from the face of the elect.

Chapter 55

Seferim Khanok

1 After this I beheld another army of chariots with men riding in them.

2 And they came upon the wind from the east, from the west, and from the south.

3 The sound of the noise of their chariots was heard.

4 And when that agitation took place; the kedushim out of shamayim perceived it; the pillar of the eretz shook from its foundation; and the sound was heard from the extremities of the eretz unto the extremities of shamayim at the same time.

5 Then they all fell down, and worshipped the Master of ruakhot.

6 This is the end of the second parable.

Chapter 56
1 I now began to utter the third parable, concerning the kedushim and the elect.

2 Benevolent are you, O kedushim and elect, for esteemed is your lot.

3 The kedushim shall exist in the light of the sun, and the elect in the light of everlasting life, the days of whose life shall never terminate; nor shall the days of the kedushim be numbered, who seek for light, and obtain right-ruling with the Master of ruakhot.

4 Shalom be to the kedushim with the Master of the world.

5 Hence forward shall the kedushim be told to seek in shamayim the secrets of right-ruling, the portion of faith; for like the sun has it arisen upon the eretz, while darkness has passed away. There shall be light interminable; nor shall they enter upon the enumeration of time; for darkness shall be previously destroyed, and light shall increase before the Master of ruakhot; before the Master of ruakhot shall the light of uprightness increase for ever.

Seferim Khanok

Chapter 57

1 In those days my eyes beheld the secrets of the lightnings and the splendors, and the judgment belonging to them.

2 They lighten for an increase and for a curse, according to the will of the Master of ruakhot.

3 And there I saw the secrets of the thunder, when it rattles above in shamayim, and its sound is heard.

4 The habitations also of the eretz were shown to me. The sound of the thunder is for shalom and for increase, as well as for a curse, according to the word of the Master of ruakhot.

5 Afterwards every secret of the splendors and of the lightnings was seen by me. For increase and for fertility they lighten.

Chapter 58

1 In the five hundredth year, and in the seventh month, on the fourteenth *day* of the month, of the lifetime of Khanok, in that parable, I saw that the shamayim of shamayim shook; that it shook violently; and that the powers of the Most High, and the malakhim, thousands and thousands, and myriads of myriads, were agitated with great agitation. And when I looked, the Ancient of days was sitting on the throne of his esteem, while the malakhim and kedushim were standing around him. A great trembling came upon me, and terror seized me. My loins were bowed down and loosened; my reins were dissolved; and I fell upon my face.[1] The set-apart Micha'el, another set-apart malakh, one of the set-apart ones, was sent, who raised me up.

2 And when he raised me, my ruakh returned; for I was incapable of enduring this vision of violence, its agitation, and the concussion of shamayim.

---

[1] All Patriarchs and prophets fell forward when the presence of the Holy one was visible but most Christians are ending up falling backwards since they are affected by the demonic and not the holy. Falling back is a sign of judgment in scripture which is due to most Christians for lawlessness.

Seferim Khanok

3 Then set-apart Micha'el said to me, why are you disturbed at this vision?

4 Hitherto has existed the day of mercy; and he has been merciful and long suffering towards all who dwell upon the eretz.

5 But when the time shall come, then *shall* the power, the punishment, and the judgment *take place*, which the Master of ruakhot has prepared for those who prostrate themselves to the judgment of right-ruling, for those who abjure that judgment, and for those who take *his* name in vain.[1]

6 That day has been prepared for the elect *as a day of* covenant; and for transgressors *as a day of* inquisition.

7 In that day shall be distributed *for food* two monsters; a female monster, whose name is Leviathan,[2] dwelling in the depths of the sea, above the springs of waters;

8 And a male *monster*, whose name is Behemoth; which possesses, *moving* on his breast, the invisible wilderness.

9 His name was Dendayen in the east of the garden, where the elect and the tsadik will dwell; where he received *it* from my ancestor, who was man, from Ahdahm the first of men, whom the Master of ruakhot made.

10 Then I asked of another malakh to show me the power of those monsters, how they became separated, how they became separated on the same day, one *being* in the depths of the sea, and one in the dry desert.

11 And he said, You, son of man, are here desirous of understanding secret things.

---

[1] To disobey Him and misuse and misapply and or falsify his name by adding it with other deities of the world.
[2] The type of Lilith. She became the female sea monster. See Gen 3:1 Hidden-Truths Hebraic Scrolls Bible.

Seferim Khanok

12 And the malakh of shalom, who was with me, said, these two monsters are by the power of Elohim prepared to become food, that the punishment of Elohim may not be in vain.

13 Then shall children be slain with their mothers, and sons with their fathers.

14 And when the punishment of the Master of ruakhot shall continue, upon them shall it continue that the punishment of the Master of ruakhot may not take place in vain. After that, judgment shall exist with mercy and long suffering.[1]

Chapter 59
1 Then another malakh, who proceeded with me, spoke to me;

2 And showed me the first and last secrets in shamayim above, and in the depths of the eretz:

3 In the extremities of shamayim, and in the foundations of it, and in the receptacle of the winds.

4 *He showed me* how their ruakhot were divided; how they were balanced; and how both the springs and the winds were numbered according to the force of their ruakh.

5 *He showed me* the power of the moon's light, that its power is a just one; as well as the divisions of the stars, according to their respective names;

6 *That* every division is divided; that the lightning flashes;

7 That its troops immediately obey; and that a cessation takes place during thunder in continuance of its sound. Nor are the thunder and the lightning separated; neither do both of them move with one ruakh; yet they are not separated.

---

[1] Lawless people will be thrown in the desert and these monsters let loose to inflict judgment upon them. One portion of people will be thrown in the desert and one portion in the sea where these two monsters will be active so there will be no escape for the unrighteous that includes Torah breaking Christians.

8 For when the lightning lightens, the thunder sounds, and the ruakh at a proper period pauses, making an equal division between them; for the receptacle, upon which their periods depend, is *loose* as sand. Each of them at a proper season is restrained with a bridle; and turned by the power of the ruakh, which thus propels *them* according to the spacious extent of the eretz.

9 The ruakh likewise of the sea is potent and strong; and as a strong power causes it to ebb, so is it driven forwards, and scattered against the mountains of the eretz. The ruakh of the frost has its malakh; in the ruakh of hail there is a good malakh; the ruakh of snow ceases in its strength, and a solitary ruakh is in it, which ascends from it like vapor and is called refrigeration.

10 The ruakh also of mist dwells with them in their receptacle; but it has a receptacle to itself; for its progress is in splendor.

11 In light, and in darkness, in winter and in summer. Its receptacle is bright, and a malakh is *in it*.

12 The ruakh of dew *has* its abode in the extremities of shamayim, in connection with the receptacle of rain; and its progress is in winter and in summer. The cloud produced by it, and the cloud of the mist, become united; one gives to the other; and when the ruakh of rain is in motion from its receptacle, malakhim come, and opening its receptacle, bring it forth.

13 When likewise it is sprinkled over all the eretz, it forms a union with every kind of mayim on the ground; for the waters remain on the ground, because *they afford* nourishment to the eretz from the Most High, who is in shamayim.

14 Upon this account therefore there is a regulation in the quantity of rain, which the malakhim receive.

15 These things I saw; all of them, even paradise.

Chapter 60

Seferim Khanok

1 In those days I beheld long ropes given to those malakhim; who took to their wings, and fled, advancing towards the north.

2 And I inquired of the malakh, saying, Why have they taken those long ropes, and gone forth? He said, They are gone forth to measure.

3 The malakh, who proceeded with me, said, These are the measures of the tsadik; and cords shall the tsadik bring, that they may trust in the name of the Master of ruakhot for ever and ever.

4 The elect shall begin to dwell with the elect.

5 And these are the measures which shall be given to faith, and *which* shall strengthen the words of right-ruling.

6 These measures shall reveal all the secrets in the depth of the eretz.

7 And *it shall be*, that those who have been destroyed in the desert, and who have been devoured by the fish of the sea, and by wild beasts, shall return, and trust in the day of the Elect One; for none shall perish in the presence of the Master of ruakhot, nor shall any be capable of perishing.

8 Then they received the commandment, all *who were* in the shamayim above; to whom a combined power, voice, and splendor, like fire, were given.

9 And first, with *their* voice, they magnified him, they exalted him, they esteemed him with wisdom, and ascribed to him wisdom with the word, and with the breath of life.

10 Then the Master of ruakhot seated upon the throne of his esteem the Elect One;

11 Who shall judge all the works of the set-apart, in shamayim above, and in a balance shall he weigh their actions. And when he shall lift up his countenance to judge their secret ways in the word of the name of the Master of ruakhot, and their progress in the path of the tsadik judgment of Elohim most high;

12 They shall all speak with united voice; and Benevolent, glorify, exalt, and praise, in the name of the Master of ruakhot.

13 He shall call to every power of the shamayim, to all the set-apart above, and to the power of Elohim. The Cherubim, the Seraphim, and the Ophanin all the malakhim of power, and all the malakhim of the Masters, namely, of the Elect One, and of the other Power, who *was* upon eretz over the mayim on that day,

14 Shall raise their united voice; shall speak benevolent, to glorify, praise, and exalt with the ruakh of faith, with the ruakh of wisdom and patience, with the ruakh of mercy, with the ruakh of judgment and shalom, and with the ruakh of benevolence; all shall say with united voice; Benevolent is He; and the name of the Master of ruakhot shall be benevolent for ever and for ever; all, who sleep not, shall say increases of it in shamayim above.

15 All the set-apart in shamayim shall exalt it; all the elect who dwell in the garden of life; and every ruakh of light, who is capable of magnifying, glorifying, exalting, and praising your set-apart name; and every mortal man, more than the powers *of shamayim*, shall glorify and exalt your name for ever and ever.

16 For great is the mercy of the Master of ruakhot; long-suffering is he; and all his works, all his power, great as are the things which he has done, has he revealed to the kedushim and to the elect, in the name of the Master of ruakhot.

Chapter 61
1 Thus YHWH commanded the kings, the princes, the exalted, and those who dwell on eretz, saying, Open your eyes, and lift up your horns, if you are capable of comprehending the Elect One.

2 YHWH of ruakhot sat upon the throne of his esteem.

Seferim Khanok

3 And the ruakh of right-ruling was poured out over him.

4 The word of his mouth shall destroy all the transgressors and all the ungodly, who shall perish at his presence.

5 In that day shall all the kings, the princes, the exalted, and those who possess the eretz, stand up, behold, and perceive, that he is sitting on the throne of his esteem; that before him the kedushim shall be judged in right-ruling;

6 And that nothing, which shall be spoken before him, shall be *spoken* in vain.

7 Trouble shall come upon them, as upon a woman in travail, whose labour is severe, when her child comes to the mouth of the womb, and she finds it difficult to bring forth.

8 One portion of them shall look upon another. They shall be astonished, and shall humble their countenance;

9 And trouble shall seize them, when they shall behold this Son of woman sitting upon the throne of his esteem.

10 Then shall the kings, the princes, and all who possess the eretz, glorify him who has dominion over all things, him who was concealed; for from the beginning the Son of man existed in secret, whom the Most High preserved in the presence of his power, and revealed to the elect.

11 He shall sow the congregation of the kedushim, and of the elect; and all the elect shall stand before him in that day.

12 All the kings, the princes, the exalted, and those who rule over all the eretz, shall fall down on their faces before him, and shall worship him.

13 They shall fix their hopes on this Son of man, shall petition to him, and petition him for mercy.

14 Then shall the Master of ruakhot hasten to expel them from his presence. Their faces shall be full of confusion,

Seferim Khanok

and their faces shall darkness cover. The malakhim shall take them to punishment, that vengeance may be inflicted on those who have oppressed his children and his elect. And they shall become an example to the kedushim and to his elect. Through them shall these be made joyful; for the anger of the Master of ruakhot shall rest upon them.[1]

15 Then the sword of the Master of ruakhot shall be drunk with their blood; but the kedushim and elect shall be safe in that day; nor the face of the transgressors and the ungodly shall they thenceforwards behold.

16 The Master of ruakhot shall remain over them:

17 And with this Son of man shall they dwell, eat, lie down, and rise up, for ever and ever.

18 The kedushim and the elect have arisen from the eretz, have left off to depress their countenances, and have been clothed with the garment of life. That garment of life is with the Master of ruakhot, in whose presence your garment shall not wax old, nor shall your esteem diminish.

Chapter 62

1 In those days the kings who possess the eretz shall be punished by the malakhim of his wrath, wheresoever they shall be delivered up, that he may give rest for a short period; and that they may fall down and worship before the Master of ruakhot, confessing their sins before him.[2]

2 They shall exalt and glorify the Master of ruakhot, saying, Benevolent is the Master of ruakhot, the Master of kings, the Master of princes, the Master of the rich, the Master of esteem, and the Master of wisdom.

3 He shall enlighten every secret thing.

---

[1] These will be punished for their disbelief.

[2] These were the kings who subjugates and enslaved his people. Enoch was a black man who lived in the region of Nok hence Cha-nok a region in West Africa. He is here speaking about the evils these kings did to the Black people who were the true Jews.

Seferim Khanok

4 Your power is from generation to generation; and your esteem for ever and ever.

5 Deep are all your secrets, and numberless; and your right-ruling cannot be calculated.

6 Now we know, that we should glorify and exalt the Master of kings, him who is King over all things.

7 They shall also say, Who has granted us rest to glorify, laud, exalt, and confess in the presence of his esteem?

8 And now small is the rest we desire; but we do not find *it*; we reject, and do not possess *it*. Light has passed away from before us; and darkness *has covered* our thrones for ever.

9 For we have not confessed before him; we have not esteemed the name of the Master of kings; we have not esteemed the Master in all his works; but we have trusted in the sceptre of our dominion and of our esteem.

10 In the day of our suffering and of our trouble he will not save us, neither shall we find rest. We confess that our Master is faithful in all his works, in all his judgments, and in his right-ruling.

11 In his judgments he pays no respect to persons; and we must depart from his presence, on account of our *evil* deeds.

12 All our sins are truly without number.

13 Then shall they say to themselves, Our souls are satiated with the instruments of crime;

14 But that prevents us not from descending to the flaming womb of hell.

15 Afterwards, their countenances shall be filled with darkness and confusion before the Son of man; from whose presence they shall be expelled, and before whom the sword shall remain to expel them.

Seferim Khanok

16 Thus says the Master of ruakhot, This is the decree and the judgment against the princes, the kings, the exalted, and those who possess the eretz, in the presence of the Master of ruakhot.

Chapter 63

1 I saw also other countenances in that secret place. I heard the voice of a malakh, saying, These are the malakhim who have descended from shamayim to eretz, and have revealed secrets to the sons of men, and have seduced the sons of men to the commission of transgression.

Chapter 64

1 In those days Noakh saw that the eretz became inclined, and that destruction approached.[1]

2 Then he lifted up his feet, and went to the ends of the eretz, to the dwelling of his great-grandfather Khanok.

3 And Noakh cried with a bitter voice, Hear me; hear me; hear me: three times. And he said, Tell me what is transacting upon the eretz; for the eretz labours, and is violently shaken. Surely I shall perish with it.

4 After this there was a great perturbation on eretz, and a voice was heard from shamayim. I fell down on my face, when my great-grandfather Khanok came and stood by me.

5 He said to me, Why have you cried out to me with a bitter cry and lamentation?

6 A commandment has gone forth from the Master against those who dwell on the eretz, that they may be destroyed; for they know every secret of the malakhim, every oppressive and secret power of the devils, and every power of those who commit sorcery, as well as of those who make molten *images* in the whole eretz.

---

[1] Chapters 64-67 are visions of Noach and not Khanok.

Seferim Khanok

7 *They know* how silver is produced from the dust of the eretz, and how on the eretz the *metallic* drop exists; for lead and tin are not produced from eretz, as the primary fountain of their production.

8 There is a malakh standing upon it, and that malakh struggles to prevail.

9 Afterwards my great-grandfather Khanok seized me with his hand, raising me up, and saying to me, Go, for I have asked the Master of ruakhot respecting this perturbation of the eretz; who replied, On account of their impiety have their innumerable judgments been consummated before me. Because of their sorceries which they have learnt, and they have known that the eretz will be destroyed with those who dwell upon it, and that to these there will be *no place of* refuge for ever.

10 They have discovered secrets, and *they are* those who have been judged; but not you my son. The Master of ruakhot knows that you are pure and good, *free* from the reproach of *discovering* secrets.

11 He, the set-apart One, will establish your name in the midst of the kedushim, and will preserve you from those who dwell upon the eretz. He will establish your seed in right-ruling, with dominion and great esteem; and from your seed shall spring forth right-ruling and set-apart men without number for ever.

Chapter 65
1 After this he showed me the malakhim of punishment, who were prepared to come, and to open all the mighty waters under the eretz:

2 That they may be for judgment, and for the destruction of all those who remain and dwell upon the eretz.

3 And the Master of ruakhot commanded the malakhim who went forth, not to take up the men and preserve *them*.

4 For those malakhim *presiding* over all the mighty waters. Then I went out from the presence of Khanok.

Seferim Khanok

Chapter 66

1 In those days the word of Elohim came to me, and said, Noakh, behold, your lot has ascended up to me, a lot void of crime, a lot beloved and upright.

2 Now then shall the malakhim labour at the etzim; but when they proceed to this, I will put my hand upon it, and preserve it.

3 The seed of life shall arise from it, and a change shall take place, that the dry land shall not be left empty. I will establish your seed before me for ever and ever, and the seed of those who dwell with you on the surface of the eretz. It shall be increased and multiplied in the presence of the eretz, in the name of the Master.

4 And they shall confine those malakhim who disclosed impiety. In that burning valley *it is, that they shall be confined*, which at first my great-grandfather Khanok showed me in the west, where there were mountains of gold and silver, of iron, of fluid metal, and of tin.[1]

5 I beheld that valley in which there was great perturbation, and *where* the waters were troubled.

6 And when all this was affected, from the fluid mass of fire, and the perturbation which prevailed in that place, there arose a strong smell of sulphur, which became mixed with the waters; and the valley of the malakhim, who had been guilty of seduction, burned underneath its soil.

7 Through that valley also rivers of fire were flowing, to which those malakhim shall be condemned, who seduced the inhabitants of the eretz.

8 And in those days shall these waters be to kings, to princes, to the exalted, and to the inhabitants of the eretz, for the healing of the soul and body, and for the judgment of the ruakh.

---

[1] These are confined in Saudi Arabia and under West Africa bound in chains.

Seferim Khanok

9 Their ruakhot shall be full of revelry, that they may be judged in their bodies; because they have denied YHWH of ruakhot, and *although* they perceive their condemnation day by day, they believe not in his name.

10 And as the inflammation of their bodies shall be great, so shall their ruakhot undergo a change for ever.

11 For no word which is uttered before the Master of ruakhot shall be in vain.

12 Judgment has come upon them, because they trusted in their carnal revelry, and denied the Master of ruakhot.

13 In those days shall the waters of that valley be changed; for when the *rebellious* malakhim shall be judged, then shall the heat of those springs of mayim experience an alteration.

14 And when the malakhim shall ascend, the mayim of the springs shall *again* undergo a change, and be frozen. Then I heard set-apart Micha'el answering and saying, This judgment, with which the *rebellious* malakhim shall be judged, shall bear testimony against the kings, the princes, and those who possess the eretz.

15 For these waters of judgment shall be for their healing, and for the death of their bodies. But they shall not perceive and believe that the waters will be changed, and become a fire, which shall blaze for ever.

Chapter 67
1 After this he gave me the signs of all the secret things in the book of my great-grandfather Khanok, and in the parables which had been given to him; inserting them for me among the words of the book of parables.

2 At that that time set-apart Micha'el answered and said to Raphael, The power of the ruakh hurries me away, and impels me on. The severity of the judgment, of the secret judgment of the malakhim, who is capable *of beholding*– the endurance of that severe judgment which has taken place and been made permanent–without being melted at

Seferim Khanok

the site of it? Again set-apart Micha'el answered and said to set-apart Raphael, Who is there whose heart is not softened by it, and whose reins are not troubled at this thing?

3 Judgment has gone forth against them by those who have thus dragged them away; and that was, when they stood in the presence of the Master of ruakhot.

4 In like manner also set-apart Rakael said to Raphael, They shall not be before the eye of the Master; since the Master of ruakhot has been offended with them; for like kings have they conducted themselves. Therefore will he bring upon them a secret judgment for ever and ever.

5 For neither shall malakh nor man receive a portion of it; but they alone shall receive their own judgment for ever end ever.

Chapter 68
1 After this judgment they shall be astonished and irritated; for it shall be exhibited to the inhabitants of the eretz.

2 Behold the names of those *rebellious* malakhim. These are their names. The first of them is Shemyaza; the second, Arstikapha; the third, Armen; the fourth, Kakabael; the fifth, Turiel; the sixth, Rumyel; the seventh, Danyal; the eighth, Kael; the ninth, Barakel; the tenth, Azazel; the eleventh, Armers; the twelfth, Bataryal; the thirteenth, Basasael; the fourteenth, Ananel; the fifteenth, Turyal; the sixteenth, Simapiseel; the seventeenth, Yetarel; the eighteenth, Tumael; the nineteenth, Tarel; the twentieth, Rumel; the twenty-first, Azazyel.

3 These are the chiefs of their malakhim, and the names of the leaders of their hundreds, and the leaders of their fifties, and the leaders of their tens.

Seferim Khanok

4 The name of the first is Yekun[1] he it was who seduced all the sons of the set-apart malakhim; and causing them to descend on eretz, led astray the offspring of men.

5 The name of the second is Kesabel, who pointed out evil counsel to the sons of the set-apart malakhim, and induced them to corrupt their bodies by generating mankind.

6 The name of the third is Gadri'el : he discovered every stroke of death to the children of men.

7 He seduced Khawa (Eve);[2] and made known to the children of men the instruments of death, the coat of mail, the shield, and the sword for slaughter; every instrument of death to the children of men.

8 From his hand were *these things* derived to them who dwell upon eretz, from that period for ever.

9 The name of the fourth is Penemue: he discovered to the children of men bitterness and sweetness;

10 And pointed out to them every secret of their wisdom.

11 He taught men to understand writing, and *the use of* ink and paper.

12 Therefore numerous have been those who have gone astray from every period of the world, even to this day.

13 For men were not born for this, thus with pen and with ink to confirm their faith;

---

[1] The rebel angel.
[2] According to Enoch Gadriel seduced Chava at the command of haStan himself as the serpent therefore Elohim punished both the one doing the crime and the one who instigated it such as Satan. However in reality Gadri'el was only part of the fallen angels who were part of the conspiracy however the leader was Shemyaza who made a pact with Lilith the first woman who helped to deceive Chava. Gadri'el was a typically a blacksmith master of iron. He helped to seduce Chava's children on an ongoing basis.

14 Since they were not created, except that, like the malakhim, they might remain tsadik and pure.

15 Nor would death, which destroys everything, have affected them;

16 But by this their knowledge they perish, and by this also *its* power consumes *them*.

17 The name of the fifth is Kasyade: he revealed to the children of men every wicked stroke of ruakhot and of demons:

18 The stroke of the embryo in the womb, for its miscarriage; the stroke of the ruakh *by* the bite of the serpent, and the stroke which is *given* in the mid-day *by* the offspring of the serpent, the name of which is Tabaet.

19 This is the number of the Kasbel; the principal part of the oath which the Most High, dwelling in esteem, revealed to the set-apart ones.

20 Its name is Beka. He spoke to set-apart Micha'el to discover to them the sacred name, that they might understand that secret name, and thus remember the oath; and that those who pointed out every secret thing to the children of men might tremble at that name and oath.

21 This is the power of that oath; for powerful it is, and strong.

22 And he established this oath of Akae by the instrumentality of the set-apart Micha'el.

23 These are the secrets of this oath, and by it were they confirmed.

24 Shamayim was suspended *by it* before the world was made, for ever.

25 By it has the eretz been founded upon the flood; while from the concealed parts of the hills the agitated waters proceed forth from the creation to the end of the world.

Seferim Khanok

26 By this oath the sea has been formed, and the foundation of it.

27 During the period of *its* fury he established the sand against it, which continues unchanged for ever; and by this oath the abyss has been made strong; nor is it removable from its station for ever and ever.

28 By this oath the sun and moon complete their progress, never swerving from the command *given* to them for ever and ever.

29 By this oath the stars complete their progress;

30 And when their names are called, they return an answer, for ever and ever.

31 Thus *in* the shamayim *take place* the blowing of the winds: all of them have breathings, and *effect* a complete combination of breathings.

32 There the treasures of thunder are kept, and the splendor of the lightning.

33 There are kept the treasures of hail and of frost, the treasures of snow, the treasures of rain and of dew.

34 All these confess and laud before the Master of ruakhot.

35 They glorify with all their power of praise; and he sustains them in all that *act of* thanksgiving; while they laud, glorify, and exalt the name of the Master of ruakhot for ever and ever.

36 And with them he establishes this oath, by which they and their paths are preserved; nor does their progress perish.

37 Great was their joy.

38 They magnified, esteemed, and exalted, because the name of the Son of man was revealed to them.

Seferim Khanok

39 He sat upon the throne of his esteem; and the principal part of the judgment was assigned to him, the Son of man. Transgressors shall disappear and perish from the face of the eretz, while those who seduced them shall be bound with chains for ever.

40 According to their ranks of corruption shall they be imprisoned, and all their works shall disappear from the face of the eretz; nor thenceforward shall there be any to corrupt; for the Son of man has been seen, sitting on the throne of his esteem.

41 Everything wicked shall disappear, and depart from before his face; and the word of the Son of man shall become powerful in the presence of the Master of ruakhot.

42 This is the third parable of Khanok.

Chapter 69
1 After this the name of the Son of man, living with the Master of ruakhot, was exalted by the inhabitants of the eretz.

2 It was exalted in the chariots of the Spirit; and the name went forth in the midst of them.

3 From that time I was not drawn into the midst of them; but he seated me between two ruakhot, between the north and the west, where the malakhim received their ropes, to measure out a place for the elect and the tsadik.

4 There I beheld the fathers of the first men, and the kedushim, who dwell in that place for ever.

Chapter 70
1 Afterwards my ruakh was concealed, ascending into the shamayim. I beheld the sons of the set-apart malakhim treading on flaming fire, whose garments and robes were white, and whose countenances were transparent as crystal.

2 I saw two rivers of fire glittering like the hyacinth.

Seferim Khanok

3 Then I fell on my face before the Master of ruakhot.

4 And Micha'el, one of the chief malakhim, took me by my right hand, raised me up, and brought me out *to* where *was* every secret *of* mercy and secret *of* right-ruling.

5 He showed me all the hidden things of the extremities of shamayim, all the receptacles of the stars, and the splendors of all, from where they went forth before the face of the set-apart.

6 And he concealed the ruakh of Khanok in the shamayim of shamayim.

7 There I beheld, in the midst of that light, a building raised with stones of ice;

8 And in the midst of these stones tongues of living fire. My ruakh saw around the circle of this flaming habitation, on one of its extremities, *that there were* rivers full of living fire, which encompassed it.

9 Then the Seraphim, the Cherubim, and Ophanin[1] surrounded *it*: these are those who never sleep, but watch the throne of his esteem.

10 And I beheld malakhim innumerable, thousands of thousands, and myriads and myriads, who surrounded that habitation.

11 Micha'el, Raphael, Gabri'el, Phanuel and the set-apart malakhim who were in the shamayim above, went in and out of it. Micha'el, Raphael, and Gabri'el went out of that habitation, and set-apart malakhim innumerable.

12 With them *was* the Ancient of days, whose head *was* white as wool, and pure, and his robe *was* indescribable.

13 Then I fell upon my face, while all my flesh was dissolved, and my ruakh became changed.

---

[1] These were the wheels of Ezekiel's chariot.

Seferim Khanok

14 I cried out with a loud voice, with a powerful ruakh, magnifying, glorifying, and exalting.

15 And those increases, which proceeded from my mouth, became acceptable in the presence of the Ancient of days.

16 The Ancient of days came with Micha'el and Gabri'el, Raphael and Phanuel, with thousands of thousands, and myriads and myriads, which could not be numbered.

17 Then that malakh came to me, and with his voice greeted me, saying, You are the son of man, who is born for right-ruling, and right-ruling has rested upon you.

18 The right-ruling of the Ancient of days shall not forsake you.

19 He said, on you shall he confer shalom in the name of the existing world; for from thence has shalom gone forth since the world was created.

20 And thus shall it happen to you for ever and ever.

21 All who shall exist, and who shall walk in your path of right-ruling, shall not forsake you for ever.

22 With you shall be their habitations, with you their lot; nor from you shall they be separated for ever and ever.

23 And thus shall length of days be with the Son of man.

24 Shalom shall be to the tsadik; and the path of integrity shall the tsadik pursue, in the name of the Master of ruakhot, for ever and ever.

Chapter 71
1 The book of the revolutions[1] of the luminaries of shamayim, according to their respective classes, their respective powers, their respective periods, their respective names, the places where they commence their progress, and their respective months, which Uri'el, the

---

[1] Yearly

set-apart malakh who was with me, explained to me; he who conducted them. The whole account of them, according to every year of the world for ever, until a new work shall be effected, which will be eternal.

2 This is the first law of the luminaries. The sun *and* the light arrive at the gates of shamayim, which are on the east, and on the west of it at the western gates of shamayim.

3 I beheld the gates[1] from where the sun goes forth; and the gates where the sun sets;

4 In which gates also the moon rises and sets; and *I beheld* the conductors of the stars, among those who precede them; six *gates were* at the rising, and six at the setting of the sun.

5 All these respectively, one after another, are on a level; and numerous windows are on the right and on the left sides of those gates.

6 First proceeds forth that great luminary, which is called the sun; the orb of which is as the orb of shamayim, the whole of it being replete with splendid and flaming fire.

7 Its chariot, where it ascends, the wind blows.

8 The sun sets in shamayim, and, returning by the north, to proceed towards the east, is conducted so as to enter by that gate, and illuminate the face of shamayim.

9 In the same manner it goes forth in the first month by the great gate.

10 It goes forth through the fourth of those six gates, which are at the rising of the sun.

11 And in the fourth gate, through which the sun with the moon proceeds, in the first part of it, there are twelve open

---

[1] Not a literal door but it means an authority given to a direction.

Seferim Khanok

windows; from which issues out a flame, when they are opened in their proper periods.

12 When the sun rises in shamayim, it goes forth through this fourth gate thirty days, and by the fourth gate in the west of shamayim on a level with it descends.

13 During that period the day is lengthened from the day, and the night curtailed from the night for thirty days. And then the day is longer by two parts than the night.

14 The day is precisely ten parts, and the night is eight.

15 The sun goes forth through this fourth gate, and sets in it, and turns to the fifth gate during thirty days; after which it proceeds from, and sets in, the fifth gate.

16 Then the day becomes lengthened by a second portion, so that it is eleven parts: while the night becomes shortened, and is only seven parts.

17 The sun *now* returns to the east, entering into the sixth gate, and rising and setting in the sixth gate thirty-one days, on account of its signs.

18 At that period the day is longer than the night, being twice *as long as* the night; and become twelve parts;

19 But the night is shortened, and becomes six parts. Then the sun rises up, that the day may be shortened, and the night lengthened.

20 And the sun returns toward the east entering into the sixth gate, where it rises and sets for thirty days.

21 When that period is completed, the day becomes shortened precisely one part, so that it is eleven parts, while the night is seven parts.

22 Then the sun goes from the west, from that sixth gate, and proceeds eastwards, rising in the fifth gate for thirty days, and setting again westwards in the fifth gate of the west.

Seferim Khanok

23 At that period the day becomes shortened two parts; and is ten parts, while the night is eight parts.

24 Then the sun goes from the fifth gate, as it sets in the fifth gate of the west; and rises in the fourth gate for thirty-one days, on account of its signs, setting in the west.

25 At that period the day is made equal with the night; and, being equal with it, the night becomes nine parts, and the day nine parts.

26 Then the sun goes from that gate, as it sets in the west; and returning to the east proceeds by the third gate for thirty days, setting in the west at the third gate.

27 At that period the night is lengthened from the day during thirty mornings, and the day is curtailed from the day during thirty days; the night being ten parts precisely, and the day eight parts.

28 The sun now goes from the third gate, as it sets in the third gate in the west; but returning to the east, it proceeds by the second gate of the east for thirty days.

29 In like manner also it sets in the second gate in the west of shamayim.

30 At that period the night is eleven parts, and the day seven parts.

31 Then the sun goes at that time from the second gate, as it sets in the second gate in the west; but returns to the east, *proceeding* by the first gate, for thirty-one days.

32 And sets in the west in the first gate.

33 At that period that night is lengthened as much again as the day.

34 It is twelve parts precisely, while the day is six parts.

35 The sun has *thus* completed its beginnings, and a second time goes round from these beginnings.

36 Into that *first* gate it enters for thirty days, and sets in the west, in the opposite part *of shamayim*.

37 At that period the night is contracted in its length a fourth part, that is, one portion, and becomes eleven parts.

38 The day is seven parts.

39 Then the sun returns, and enters into the second gate of the east.

40 It returns by these beginnings thirty days, rising and setting.

41 At that period the night is contracted in its length. It becomes ten parts, and the day eight parts. Then the sun goes from that second gate, and sets in the west; but returns to the east, and rises in the east, in the third gate, thirty-one days, setting in the west of shamayim.

42 At that period the night becomes shortened. It is nine parts. And the night is equal with the day. The year is precisely three hundred and sixty-four days.

43 The lengthening of the day and night, and the contraction of the day and night, are made to differ from each other by the progress of the sun.

44 By means of this progress the day is daily lengthened, and the night greatly shortened.

45 This is the law and progress of the sun and it's turning when it turns back, turning during sixty days, and going forth. This is the great everlasting luminary, that which he names the sun for ever and ever.

46 This also is that which goes forth a great luminary, and which is named after its peculiar kind, as Elohim commanded.

47 And thus it goes in and out, neither slackening nor resting; but running on in its chariot by day and by night. It shines with a seventh portion of light from the moon; 78 but the dimensions of both are equal.

Chapter 72

1 After this law I beheld another law of an inferior luminary, the name of which is the moon, and the orb of which is as the orb of shamayim.

2 Its chariot, *which* it secretly ascends, the wind blows; and light is given to it by measure.

3 Every month at its exit and entrance it becomes changed; and its periods are as the periods of the sun. And when in like manner its light is to exist, its light is a seventh portion from the light of the sun.

4 Thus it rises, and at its commencement towards the east goes forth for thirty days.

5 At that time it appears, and becomes to you the beginning of the month. Thirty days *it is* with the sun in the gate from which the sun goes forth.

6 Half of it is in extent seven portions, one *half*; and the whole of its orb is void of light, except a seventh portion out of the fourteen portions of its light. And in a day it receives a seventh portion, or half *that portion*, of its light. Its light is by sevens, by one portion, and by the half *of a portion*. Its sets with the sun.

7 And when the sun rises, the moon rises with it; receiving half a portion of light.

8 On that night, when it commences its period, previously to the day of the month, the moon sets with the sun.

9 And on that night it is dark *in* its fourteen portions, that is, *in each* half; but it rises on that day with one seventh portion precisely, and in its progress declines from the rising of the sun.

10 During the remainder of its period its light increases to fourteen portions.

Seferim Khanok

Chapter 73

1 Then I saw another progress and regulation which He effected in the law of the moon. The progress of the moons, and everything *relating to them*, Uri'el showed me, the set-apart malakh who conducted them all.

2 Their stations I wrote down as he showed them to me.

3 I wrote down their months, as they occur, and the appearance of their light, until it is completed in fifteen days.

4 In each of its two seven portions it completes all its light at rising and at setting.

5 On stated months it changes *its* settings; and on stated months it makes its progress *through* each *gate*. In two *gates* the moon sets with the sun, *viz.* in those two gates which are in the midst, in the third and fourth gate. *From the third gate* it goes forth for seven days, and makes its circuit.

6 Again it returns to the gate whence the sun goes forth, and in that completes the whole of its light. Then it declines from the sun, and enters in eight days into the sixth gate, *and returns in seven days to the third gate*, from which the sun goes forth.

7 When the sun proceeds to the fourth gate, the *moon* goes forth for seven days, until it passes from the fifth *gate*.

8 Again it returns in seven days to the fourth gate, and completing all its light, declines, and passes on by the first gate in eight days;

9 And returns in seven days to the fourth gate, from which the sun goes forth.

10 Thus I beheld their stations, as according to the fixed order of the months the sun rises and sets.

11 At those times there is an excess of thirty days belonging to the sun in five years; all the days belonging to each year of the five years, when completed, amount to three hundred and sixty-four days; and to the sun and stars belong six days; six days in each of the five years; *thus* thirty days belonging to them;

12 So that the moon has thirty days less than the sun and stars.

13 The moon brings on all the years exactly, that their stations may come neither too forwards nor too backwards a single day; but that the years may be changed with correct precision in three hundred and sixty-four days. In three years the days are one thousand and ninety-two; in five years they are one thousand eight hundred and twenty; and in eight years two thousand nine hundred and twelve days.

14 To the moon alone belong in three years one thousand and sixty-two days; in five years it has fifty days less *than the sun*, for an addition being made to the *one thousand and* sixty-two days, in five years there are one thousand seven hundred and seventy days; and the days of the moon in eight years are two thousand eight hundred and thirty-two days.

15 For its days in eight years are less *than those of the sun by* eighty days, which eighty days are its diminution in eight years.

16 The year then becomes truly complete according to the station of the moon, and the station of the sun; which rise in the *different* gates; which rise and set in them for thirty days.

Chapter 74
1 *These are* the leaders of the chiefs of the thousands, *those* which *preside* over all creation, and over all the stars; with the four *days* which are added and never separated from the place allotted them, according to the complete calculation of the year.

2 And these serve four days, which are not calculated in the calculation of the year.

Seferim Khanok

3 Respecting them, men greatly err, for these luminaries truly serve, in the dwelling place of the world, one *day* in the first gate, one in the third gate, one in the fourth gate, and one in the sixth gate.

4 And the harmony of the world becomes complete every three hundred and sixty-fourth state of it. For the signs,

5 The seasons,

6 The years,

7 And the days, Uri'el showed me; the malakh whom the Master of esteem appointed over all the luminaries.

8 Of shamayim in shamayim, and in the world; that they might rule in the face of the sky, and appearing over the eretz, become

9 Conductors of the days and nights: the sun, the moon, the stars, and all the ministers of shamayim, which make their circuit with all the chariots of shamayim.

10 Thus Uri'el showed me twelve gates open for the circuit of the chariots of the sun in shamayim, from which the rays of the sun shoot forth.

11 From these proceed heat over the eretz, when they are opened in their stated seasons. They are for the winds, and the ruakh of the dew, when in their seasons they are opened; opened in shamayim at *its* extremities.

12 Twelve gates I beheld in shamayim, at the extremities of the eretz, through which the sun, moon, and stars, and all the works of shamayim, proceed at their rising and setting.

13 Many windows also are open on the right and on the left.

14 One window at a *certain* season grows extremely hot. So also are there gates from which the stars go forth as they are commanded, and in which they set according to their number.

15 I saw likewise the chariots of shamayim, running in the world above to those gates in which the stars turn, which never set. One of these is greater than all, which goes round the whole world.

Chapter 75

1 And at the extremities of the eretz I beheld twelve gates open for all the winds, from which they proceed and blow over the eretz.[1]

2 Three of them are open in the front of shamayim, three in the west, three on the right side of shamayim, and three on the left. The first three are those which are towards the east, three are towards the north, three behind those which are upon the left, towards the south, and three on the west.

3 From four of them proceed winds of increases, and of health; and from eight proceed winds of punishment; when they are sent to destroy the eretz, and the shamayim above it, all its inhabitants, and all which are in the waters, or on dry land.

4 The first of these winds proceeds from the gate termed the eastern, through the first gate on the east, which inclines southwards. From this goes forth destruction, drought, heat, and perdition.

5 From the second gate, the middle one, proceeds equity. There issue from it rain, fruitfulness, health, and dew; and from the third gate northwards, proceed cold and drought.

6 After these proceed the south winds through three principal gates; through their first gate, which inclines eastwards, proceeds a hot wind.

7 But from the middle gate proceed grateful odour, dew, rain, health, and life.

---

[1] The twelve sons of Jacob are based on them with the twelve tribes.

8 From the third gate, which is westwards, proceed dew, rain, blight, and destruction.

9 After these are the winds to the north, which is called the sea. *They proceed* from three gates. The first seventh gate *is that* which is on the east, inclining southwards; from this proceed dew, rain, blight, and destruction. From the middle direct gate proceed rain, dew, life, and health. And from the third gate, which is westwards, inclining towards the south, proceed mist, frost, snow, rain, dew, and blight.

10 After these *in the* fourth *quarter* are the winds to the west. From the first gate, inclining northwards, proceed dew, rain, frost, cold, snow, and chill; from the middle gate proceed rain, health, and increases;

11 And from the last gate, which is southwards, proceed drought, destruction, scorching, and perdition.

12 The *account of the* twelve gates of the four quarters of shamayim is ended.

13 All their laws, all their *infliction* of punishment, and the health *produced* by them, have I explained to you, my son Metushelakh.

Chapter 76
1 The first wind is called the eastern, because it is the first.

2 The second is called the south, because the Most High there descends, and frequently there descends *he who* is magnified for ever.

3 The western wind has the name of diminution, because there all the luminaries of shamayim are diminished, and descend.

4 The fourth wind, which is named the north, is divided into three parts; one of which is for the habitation of man; another for seas of mayim, with valleys, woods, rivers, shady places, and snow; and the third part *contains* paradise.

Seferim Khanok

5 Seven high mountains I beheld, higher than all the mountains of the eretz, from which frost proceeds; while days, seasons, and years depart and pass away.

6 Seven rivers I beheld upon eretz, greater than all rivers, one of which takes its course from the west; into a great sea its mayim flows.

7 Two come from the north to the sea, their waters flowing into the sea of Reeds, on the east. And with respect to the remaining four, they take their course in the cavity of the north, *two* to their sea, the sea of Reeds, and two are poured into a great sea, where also it is said *there is* a desert.

8 Seven great islands I saw in the sea and on the eretz. Seven in the great sea.

Chapter 77
1 The names of the sun are these: one Aryares, the other Tomas.

2 The moon has four names. The first is Asonya; the second, Ebla; the third, Benase; and the fourth, Erae.

3 These are the two great luminaries, whose orbs are as the orbs of shamayim; and the dimensions of both are equal.

4 In the orb of the sun *there is* a seventh portion of light, which is added to it from the moon. By measure it is put in, until the seventh portion of *the light of* the sun is departed. They set, enter into the western gate, circuit by the north, and through the eastern gate go forth over the face of shamayim.

5 When the moon rises, it appears in shamayim; and the half of a seventh portion of light is all *which is* in it.

6 In fourteen *days* the whole of its light is completed.

Seferim Khanok

7 *By* three quintuples light is put into it, until *in* fifteen *days* its light is completed, according to the signs of the year; it has three quintuples.

8 The moon has the half of a seventh portion.

9 During its diminution on the first day its light decreases a fourteenth part; on the second day it decreases a thirteenth part; on the third day a twelfth part; on the fourth day an eleventh part; on the fifth day a tenth part; on the sixth day a ninth part; on the seventh day it decreases an eighth part; on the eighth day it decreases a seventh part; on the ninth day it decreases a sixth part; on the tenth day it decreases a fifth part; on the eleventh day it decreases a fourth part; on the twelfth day it decreases third part; on the thirteenth day it decreases a second part; on the fourteenth day it decreases a half of its seventh part; and on the fifteenth day the whole remainder of its light is consumed.

10 On stated months the moon has twenty-nine days.

11 It also has a period of twenty-eight days.

12 Uri'el likewise showed me another regulation, when light is poured into the moon,[1] how it is poured into it from the sun.

13 All the time that the moon is in progress with its light, it is poured *into it* in the presence of the sun, until *its* light is in fourteen days completed in shamayim.

14 And when it is wholly extinguished, its light is consumed in shamayim; and on the first day it is called the new moon, for on that day light is received into it.

15 It becomes precisely completed on the day that the sun descends into the west, while the moon ascends at night from the east.

---

[1] The moon gives the light of the sun and does not have its own light.

16 The moon then shines all the night, until the sun rises before it; when the moon disappears in turn before the sun.

17 Where light comes to the moon, there again it decreases, until all its light is extinguished, and the days of the moon pass away.

18 Then its orb remains solitary without light.

19 During three months it effects in thirty days *each month* its period; and during three *more* months it effects it in twenty-nine days each. *These are the times* in which it effects its decrease in its first period, and in the first gate, *namely*, in one hundred and seventy-seven days.

20 And at the time of its going forth during three months it appears thirty days each, and during three *more* months it appears twenty-nine days each.[1]

21 In the night it appears for each twenty *days* as *the face of* a man, and in the day as shamayim; for it is nothing else except its light.

Chapter 78
1 And now, my son Metushelakh, I have shown you everything; and *the account of* every ordinance of the stars of shamayim is finished.

2 He showed me every ordinance respecting these, which *takes place* at all times and in all seasons under every influence, in all years, at the arrival and under the rule of each, during every month and every week. *He showed me* also the decrease of the moon, which is effected in the sixth gate; for in that sixth gate is its light consumed.

3 From this is the beginning of the month; and its decrease is effected in the sixth gate in its period, until a hundred and seventy-seven days are completed; according to the mode of calculation by weeks, twenty-five *weeks* and two days.

---

[1] The moon cycle varies each month.

Seferim Khanok

4 *Its period* is less that that of the sun, according to the ordinance of the stars, by five days in one half year precisely.

5 When that *their* visible situation is completed. Such is the appearance and likeness of every luminary, which Uri'el, the great malakh who conducts them, showed to me.

Chapter 79

1 In those days Uri'el answered and said to me, behold, I have showed you all things, O Khanok;

2 And all things have I revealed to you. You see the sun, the moon, and those which conduct the stars of shamayim, which cause all their operations, seasons, and arrivals to return.

3 In the days of transgressors the years shall be shortened.

4 Their seed shall be backward in their prolific soil; and everything done on eretz shall be subverted, and disappear in its season. The rain shall be restrained, and shamayim shall stand still.

5 In those days the fruits of the eretz shall be late, and not flourish in their season; and in their season the fruits of the etzim shall be withheld.

6 The moon shall change its laws, and not be seen at its proper period. But in those days shall shamayim be seen; and barrenness shall take place in the borders of the great chariots in the west. *Shamayim* shall shine more than *when illuminated by* the orders of light; while many chiefs among the stars of authority shall err, perverting their ways and works.

7 Those shall not appear in their season, who commanded them, and all the classes of the stars shall be shut up against transgressors.

8 The thoughts of those who dwell on the eretz shall transgress within them; and they shall be perverted in all their ways.

9 They shall transgress, and think themselves elohim; while evil shall be multiplied among them.

10 And punishment shall come upon them, so that all of them shall be destroyed.

Seferim Khanok

Chapter 80

1 He said, O Khanok, look on the book from the tablets of the shamayim[1] has gradually brought down and, reading that which is written in it, understand every part of it.

2 Then I looked on all which was written, and understood all, reading the book and everything written in it, all the works of man;

3 And of all the children of flesh upon eretz, during the generations of the world.

4 Immediately after I magnified the Master, the King of esteem, who has thus for ever formed the whole workmanship of the world.

5 And I esteemed the Master, on account of his long-suffering and increases towards the children of the world.

6 At that time I said, increased is the man, who shall die tsadik and good, against whom no catalogue of crime has been written, and with whom iniquity is not found.[2]

7 Then those three set-apart ones caused me to approach, and placed me on the eretz, before the door of my house.

8 And they said unto me, Explain everything to Metushelakh your son; and inform all your children, that no flesh shall be justified before the Master; for he is their Creator.

9 During one year we shall leave you with your children, until you shall again recover your strength, that you may instruct your family, write these things, and explain them to all your children. But in another year they shall take you from the midst of them, and your heart shall be strengthened; for the elect shall point out right-ruling to the elect; the tsadik with the tsadik shall rejoice, congratulating

---

[1] The Torah that was inscribed on Tables of stone and also given to Musa.
[2] There are two angels on each side of man who rights all our good deeds and bad. One angel for the good and one for the bad.

each other; but the transgressors with transgressors shall die,

10 And the perverted with the perverted shall be drowned.[1]

11 Those likewise who act with right-ruling shall die on account of the works of man, and shall be gathered together on account of the works of the wicked.

12 In those days they finished conversing with me.

13 And I returned to my fellow men, magnifying the Master of universes.[2]

Chapter 81
1 Now, my son Metushelakh, all these things I speak unto you, and write for you. To you I have revealed all, and have given you books of everything.

2 Preserve, my son Metushelakh, the books written by your father; that you may reveal them to future generations.

3 Wisdom have I given you, to your children, and your posterity, that they may reveal to their children, for generations for ever, this wisdom in their thoughts; and that those who comprehend *it* may not slumber, but hear with their ears; that they may learn this wisdom, and be deemed worthy of eating *this* wholesome food.

4 Increased are all the tsadik; magnified *are* all who walk in right-ruling[3]; in whom no crime *is found*, as in transgressors, when all their days are numbered.

5 With respect to the progress of the sun in shamayim, it enters and goes out of *each* gate for thirty days, with the leaders of the thousand classes of the stars; with four[4] which are added, and appertain to the four quarters of the

---

[1] Drowned in the waters.
[2] There are many universes not just this one.
[3] Obeying Torah that even Khanok taught.
[4] one day is added at each turn of the season.

year, which conduct them, and accompany them at four periods.

6 Respecting these, men greatly err, and do not calculate them in the calculation of every age; for they greatly err respecting them; nor do men know accurately that they are in the calculation of the year. But indeed these are marked down for ever;[1] one in the first gate, one in the third, one in the fourth, and one in the sixth:

7 So that the year is completed in three hundred and sixty-four days.[2]

8 Truly has been stated, and accurately has been calculated that which is marked down; for the luminaries, the months, the fixed periods, the years, and the days, Uri'el has explained to me, and communicated to me; whom the Master of all creation, on my account, commanded according to the might of shamayim, and the power which it possesses both by night and by day to explain *the laws of* light to man, of the sun, moon, and stars, and of all the powers of shamayim, which are turned with their respective orbs.

9 This is the ordinance of the stars, which set in their places, in their seasons, in their periods, in their days, and in their months.

10 These are the names of those who conduct them, who watch and enter in their seasons, according to their ordinance in their periods, in their months, in *the times of* their influence, and in their stations.

11 Four conductors of them first enter, who separate the four quarters of the year. After these, twelve conductors of their classes, who separate the months and the year *into* three hundred and sixty-four *days*, with the leaders of a thousand, who distinguish between the days, as well as

---

[1] Khanok Calendar is the only true calendar the rest are man-made like the Jewish (proselytes from Khazaria), Gregorian are all men-made calendars.
[2] You would add 1 day to make it like the solar year of today.

between the four additional ones; which, *as* conductors, divide the four quarters of the year.

12 These leaders of a thousand are in the midst of the conductors, and the conductors are added each behind his station, and their conductors make the separation. These are the names of the conductors, who separate the four quarters of the year, who are appointed *over them*: Melkel, Helammelak,

13 Meliyal, and Narel.

14 And the names of those who conduct them are Adnarel, Yyasusal, and Yyelumeal.

15 These are the three who follow after the conductors of the classes *of stars*; each following after the three conductors of the classes, which themselves follow after those conductors of the stations, who divide the four quarters of the year.

16 In the first part of the year rises and rules Melkyas, who is named Tamani, and Zahay.

17 All the days of his influence, *during* which he rules, are ninety-one days.

18 And these are the signs of the days which are seen upon the eretz. In the days of his influence *there is* perspiration, heat, and trouble. All the etzim become fruitful; the leaf of every etz comes forth; the corn is reaped; the rose and every species of flowers blossoms in the field; and the etzim of winter are dried up.

19 These are the names of the conductors who are under them: Barkel, Zelsabel; and another additional conductor of a thousand is named Heloyalef, the days of those influence have been completed. The other conductor next after them *is* Helemmelek, whose name they call the splendid Zahay.[1]

---

[1] Golden as the sun.

Seferim Khanok

20 All the days of his light are ninety-one days.

21 These are the signs of the days upon eretz, heat and drought; while the etzim bring forth their fruits, warmed and concocted, and give their fruits to dry.

22 The flocks follow and yean. All the fruits of the eretz are collected, with everything in the fields, and the vines are trodden. This takes place during the time of his influence.

23 These are their names and orders, and *the names* of the conductors who are under them, of those who are chiefs of a thousand: Gedaeyal, Keel, Heel.

24 And the name of the additional leader of a thousand is Asphael.

25 The days of his influence have been completed.

Chapter 82

1 And now I have shown you, my son Metushelakh, every sight which I saw prior to your birth. I will relate another vision, which I saw before I was married;[1] they resemble each other.

2 The first was when I was learning a book; and the other before I was married to your mother. I saw a potent vision;

3 And on account of these things besought the Master.

4 I was lying down in the house of my grandfather Malalel, *when* I saw in a vision shamayim purifying, and snatched away.

5 And falling to the eretz, I saw likewise the eretz absorbed by a great abyss; and mountains suspended over mountains.

---

[1] Note Enoch had a wife. Enoch had two wives just as African chiefs on the North/South divide, see AF Netzarim Study Scriptures.

Seferim Khanok

6 Hills were sinking upon hills, lofty etzim were gliding off from their trunks, and were in the act of being projected, and of sinking into the abyss.

7 *Being alarmed* at these things, my voice faltered. I cried out and said, the eretz is destroyed. Then my grandfather Malalel raised me up, and said to me: Why do you thus cry out, my son? And Why thus do you lament?

8 I related to him the whole vision which I had seen. He said to me, confirmed is that which you have seen, my son;

9 And potent the vision of your dream respecting every secret transgression of the eretz. Its substance shall sink into the abyss, and a great destruction take place.

10 Now, my son, rise up; and beseech the Master of esteem for you are faithful, that a remnant may be left upon eretz, and that he would not wholly destroy it. My son, all this *calamity* upon eretz comes down from shamayim; upon eretz shall there be a great destruction.

11 Then I arose, prayed, and entreated; and wrote down my petition for the generations of the world, explaining everything to my son Metushelakh.

12 When I went down below, and looking up to shamayim, beheld the sun proceeding from the east, the moon descending to the west, a few *scattered* stars, and everything which Elohim has known from the beginning, I magnified the Master of judgment, and magnified him: because he has sent forth the sun from the chambers of the east; that, ascending and rising in the face of shamayim, it might spring up, and pursue the path which has been pointed out to it.

Chapter 83

1 I lifted up my hands in right-ruling, and magnified the set-apart, and the Great One. I spoke with the breath of my mouth, and with a tongue of flesh, which Elohim has formed for all the sons of mortal men, that with it they may speak; giving them breath, a mouth, and a tongue to converse with.

Seferim Khanok

2 Benevolent are you, O YHWH, the King, great and powerful in your greatness, Master of all the creatures of shamayim, King of kings, Elohim of the whole world, whose reign, whose kingdom, and whose majesty endure forever and ever.

3 From generation to generation shall your dominion *exist*. All the shamayim are your throne for ever, and all the eretz your footstool for ever and for ever.

4 For you have made *them*, and over all you reign. No act whatsoever exceeds your power. With your wisdom is unchangeable; nor from your throne and from your presence is it ever averted. You know all things, see and hear them; nor is anything concealed from you; for you perceive all things.

5 The malakhim of your shamayim have transgressed; and on mortal flesh shall your wrath remain, until the day of the great judgment.

6 Now then, O Elohim, Master and mighty King, I entreat you, and beseech you to grant my petition, that a posterity may be left to me on eretz, and that the whole human race may not perish;

7 That the eretz may not be left destitute, and destruction take place for ever.

8 O my Master, let the race perish from off the eretz which has offended you, but a tsadik and upright race establish for a posterity 94 for ever. Hide not your face, O Master, from the petition of your servant.

Chapter 84

1 After this I saw another dream, and explained it all to you, my son. Khanok arose and said to his son Metushelakh, To you, my son, will I speak. Hear my word; and incline your ear to the visionary dream of your father. Before I married your mother Edna, I saw a vision on my bed;

2 And behold, a cow sprung forth from the eretz;

Seferim Khanok

3 And this cow was dazzling.

4 Afterwards a female heifer sprung forth; and with it another heifer: one of them was black, and one was mahogany.

5 The black heifer then struck the mahogany one, and pursued it over the eretz.

6 From that period I could see nothing more of the mahogany heifer; but the black one increased in bulk, and a female heifer came with him.

7 After this I saw that many cows proceeded forth, resembling him, and following after him.

8 The first female young one also went out in the presence of the first cow; and sought the mahogany *colored* heifer, but found him not.

9 And she lamented with a great lamentation, while she was seeking him.

10 Then I looked until that first *cow* came to her, from which time she became silent, and ceased to lament.

11 Afterwards she calved another cow.

12 And again calved many cows and black heifers.

13 In my sleep also I perceived a bull, which in like manner grew, and became a large bull.

14 After him many cows came forth, resembling him.

15 And they began to calve many *other* similar cows, which resembled them and followed each other.

Chapter 85
1 Again I looked attentively, while sleeping, and surveyed shamayim above.

2 And behold a single star fell from shamayim.

3 Which being raised up, ate and fed among those cows.

4 After that I perceived *other* large and black cows; and behold all of them changed their stalls and pastures, while their young began to lament one with another. Again I looked in *my* vision, and surveyed shamayim; when behold I saw many stars which descended, and projected themselves from shamayim to where the first star was,

5 Into the midst of those young ones; while the cows were with them, feeding in the midst of them.

6 I looked at and observed them; when behold, they all acted after the manner of horses, and began to approach the young cows, all of whom became pregnant, and brought forth elephants, camels, and asses.

7 At these all the cows were alarmed and terrified; when they began biting with their teeth, swallowing, and striking with their horns.

8 They began also to devour the cows; and behold all the children of the eretz trembled, shook with terror at them, and suddenly fled away.

Chapter 86
1 Again I perceived them, when they began to strike and to swallow each other; and the eretz cried out. Then I raised my eyes a second time towards shamayim, and saw in a vision, that, behold, there came forth from shamayim as it were the likeness of esteemed men. One came forth from thence, and three with him.

2 Those three, who came forth last, seized me by my hand; and raising me up from the generations of the eretz, elevated me to a high station.

3 Then they showed me a lofty tower on the eretz, while every hill became diminished. And they said, Remain here, until you perceive what shall come upon those elephants, camels, and asses, upon the stars, and upon all the cows.

Seferim Khanok

Chapter 87

1 Then I looked at that one of the four, who came forth first.

2 He seized the first star[1] which fell down from shamayim.

3 And, binding it hand and foot, he cast it into a valley; a valley narrow, deep, stupendous, and gloomy.

4 Then one of them drew his sword, and gave it to the elephants, camels, and asses who began to strike each other. And the whole eretz shook on account of them.

5 And when I looked in the vision, behold, one of those four malakhim, who came forth, hurled from shamayim, collected together, and took all the great stars, whose form partly resembles that of horses; and binding them all hand and foot, cast them into the cavities of the eretz.

Chapter 88

1 Then one of those four went to the cows, and taught them a mystery. While the cow was trembling, it was born, and became a man, and made for himself a large ship. In this he dwelt, and three cows dwelt with him in that ship, which covered them.[2]

2 Again I lifted up my eyes towards shamayim, and saw a lofty roof. Above it were seven cataracts, which poured fourth on a certain village much mayim.

3 Again I looked, and behold there were fountains open on the eretz in that large village.

4 The mayim began to boil up, and rose over the eretz; so that the village was not seen, while its whole soil was covered with mayim.

5 Much mayim was over it, darkness, and clouds. Then I surveyed the height of this mayim; and it was elevated above the village.

---

[1] Rebellious angel.
[2] Noah, Ham, Shem and Japheth.

Seferim Khanok

6 It flowed over the village, and stood higher than the eretz.

7 Then all the cows which were collected there, while I looked on them, were drowned, swallowed up, and destroyed in the mayim.

8 But the ship floated above it. All the cows, the elephants, the camels, and the asses, were drowned on the eretz, and all cattle. Nor could I perceive them. Neither were they able to get out, but perished, and sunk into the deep.[1]

9 Again I looked in the vision until those cataracts from that lofty roof were removed, and the fountains of the eretz became equalized, while other depths were opened;

10 Into which the mayim began to descend, until the dry ground appeared.

11 The ship remained on the eretz; the darkness receded; and it became light.

12 Then the white cow,[2] which became a man, went out of the ship and the three cows with him.

13 One of the three cows was white, resembling that cow; one of them was the colour of mahogany; and one of them was black. And the white cow left them.

14 Then began wild beasts and birds to bring forth.

15 Of all these the different kinds assembled together, lions, tigers, wolves, dogs, wild boars, foxes, rabbits, and the hanzar.

16 The siset, the avest, kites, the phonkas, and ravens.

17 Then the dazzling cow was born in the midst of them.

---

[1] The great flood of Noah.
[2] Noah though born to a black African family was of white colour an albino.

Seferim Khanok

18 And they began to bite each other; when the dazzling cow, which was born in the midst of them, brought forth a wild ass and a cow at the same time, and *after that* many wild asses. Then the cow, which was born, brought forth a black wild sow and a dazzling sheep.

19 That wild sow also brought forth many swine.

20 And that sheep brought forth twelve sheep.

21 When those twelve sheep grew up, they delivered one of them to the asses.

22 Again those asses delivered that sheep to the wolves

23 And he grew up in the midst of them.

24 Then the Master brought the eleven *other* sheep, that they might dwell and feed with him in the midst of the wolves.

25 They multiplied, and there was abundance of pasture for them.

26 But the wolves began to frighten and oppress them, while they destroyed their young ones.

27 And they left their young in torrents of deep mayim.

28 Now the sheep began to cry out on account of their young, and fled for refuge to their master. One however, which was saved, escaped, and went away to the wild asses.

29 I beheld the sheep moaning, crying, and petitioning their master.

30 With all their might, until the Master of the sheep descended at their voice from *his* lofty habitation; went to them; and inspected them.

Seferim Khanok

31 He called to that sheep which had secretly stolen away from the wolves, and told him to make the wolves understand that they were not to touch the sheep.

32 Then that sheep went to the wolves with the word of the Master, when another met him, and proceeded with him.

33 Both of them together entered the dwelling of the wolves; and conversing with them made them understand, that thenceforwards they were not to touch the sheep.

34 Afterwards I perceived the wolves greatly prevailing over the sheep with their whole force. The sheep cried out; and their Master came to them.

35 He began to strike the wolves, which commenced a grievous lamentation; but the sheep were silent, nor from that time did they cry out.

36 I then looked at them, until they departed from the wolves. The eyes of the wolves were blind, who went out and followed them with all their might. But the Master of the sheep proceeded with them, and conducted them.

37 All his sheep followed him.

38 His countenance *was* terrific and splendid, and esteemed was his aspect. Yet the wolves began to follow the sheep, until they overtook them in a certain lake of mayim.

39 Then that lake became divided; the mayim standing up on both sides before their face.[1]

40 And while their Master was conducting them, he placed himself between them and the wolves.

41 The wolves however perceived not the sheep, but went into the midst of the lake, following them, and running after them into the lake of mayim.

---

[1] The waters of the Sea of Reeds froze on both sides standing upright.

Seferim Khanok

42 But when they saw the Master of the sheep, they turned to fly from before his face.

43 Then the mayim of the lake returned, and that suddenly, according to its nature. It became full, and was raised up, until it covered the wolves. And I saw that all of them which had followed the sheep perished, and were drowned.

44 But the sheep passed over this mayim, proceeding to a wilderness, which was without both mayim and grass. And they began to open their eyes and to see.

45 Then I beheld the Master of the sheep inspecting them, and giving them mayim and grass.

46 The sheep *already mentioned* was proceeding *with them*, and conducting them.

47 And when he had ascended the top of the lofty rock, the Master of the sheep sent him to them.

48 Afterwards I perceived their Master standing before them, with an aspect terrific and severe.

49 And when they all beheld him, they were frightened at his countenance.

50 All of them were alarmed, and trembled. They cried out after that sheep; and to the other sheep who had been with him, and who was in the midst of them, *saying*, we are not able to stand before our Master, or to look upon him.

51 Then that sheep who conducted them went away, and ascended the top of the rock;

52 When the *rest of the* sheep began to grow blind, and to wander from the path which he had shown them; but he knew it not.

53 Their Master however was moved with great indignation against them; and when that sheep had learned *what had happened*,

Seferim Khanok

54 He descended from the top of the rock, and coming to them, found that there were many,

55 Which had become blind;

56 And had wandered from his path. As soon as they beheld him, they feared, and trembled at his presence;

57 And became desirous of returning to their fold,

58 Then that sheep, taking with him other sheep, went to those which had wandered.

59 And afterwards began to kill them. They were terrified at his countenance. Then he caused those which had wandered to return; who went back to their fold.

60 I likewise saw there in the vision, that this sheep became a man, built a tabernacle for the Master of the sheep, and made them all stand in the house.

61 I perceived also that the sheep which proceeded to meet this sheep, their conductor, died. I saw, too, that all the great sheep perished, while smaller ones rose up in their place, entered into a pasture, and approached a river of mayim.

62 Then that sheep, their conductor, who became a man, was separated from them, and died.

63 All the sheep sought after him, and cried for him with bitter lamentation.

64 I saw likewise that they ceased to cry after that sheep, and passed over the river of mayim.

65 And that there arose other sheep, all of whom conducted them, instead of those who were dead, and who had *previously* conducted them.

66 Then I saw that the sheep entered into a goodly place, and a territory delectable and esteemed.

Seferim Khanok

67 I saw also that they became satiated; that their house was in the midst of a delectable territory; and that sometimes their eyes were opened, and that sometimes they were blind; until another sheep[1] arose and conducted them. He brought them all back; and their eyes were opened.

68 Then dogs, foxes, and wild boars began to devour them, until *again* another sheep[2] arose, the master of the flock, one of themselves, a ram, to conduct them. This ram began to butt on every side those dogs, foxes, and wild boars, until they all perished.

69 his eyes, and saw the ram in the midst of them, who had laid aside his esteem.

70 And he began to strike the sheep, treading upon them, and behaving himself without dignity.

71 Then their Master sent the *former* sheep *again* to a still different sheep and raised him up to be a ram,[3] and to conduct them instead of that sheep who had laid aside his esteem.

72 Going therefore to him, and conversing with him alone, he raised up that ram, and made him a prince and leader of the flock. All the time that the dogs troubled the sheep,

73 The first ram paid respect to this latter ram.

74 Then the latter ram arose, and fled away from before his face. And I saw that those dogs[4] caused the first ram to fall.

75 But the latter ram arose, and conducted the smaller sheep.

76 That ram likewise begat many sheep, and died.

---

[1] Prophet Shemuel.
[2] King Shaul.
[3] King David.
[4] Philistines.

Seferim Khanok

77 Then there was a smaller sheep, a ram,[1] instead of him, which became a prince and leader, conducting the flock.

78 And the sheep increased in size, and multiplied.

79 And all the dogs, foxes, and wild boars feared, and fled away from him.

80 That ram also struck and killed all the wild beasts, so that they could not again prevail in the midst of the sheep, nor at any time ever snatch them away.

81 And that house was made large and wide; a lofty tower being built upon it by the sheep, for the Master of the sheep.

82 The house was low, but the tower was elevated and very high.

83 Then the Master of the sheep stood upon that tower, and caused a full table to approach before him.

84 Again I saw that those sheep wandered, and went various ways, forsaking that their house;

85 And that their Master called to some among them, whom he sent to them.

86 But these the sheep began to kill. And when one of them was saved from slaughter he leaped, and cried out against those who were desirous of killing him.

87 But the Master of the sheep delivered him from their hands, and made him ascend to him, and remain with him.

88 He sent also many others to them, to testify, and with lamentations to exclaim against them.

89 Again I saw, when some of them forsook the house of their Master, and his tower; wandering on all sides, and growing blind,

---

[1] King Solomon.

Seferim Khanok

90 I saw that the Master of the sheep made a great slaughter among them in their pasture, until they cried out to him in consequence of that slaughter. Then he departed from the place *of his habitation*, and left them in the power of lions, tigers, wolves, and the Hyenas, and in the power of foxes, and of every beast.

91 And the wild beasts began to tear them.

92 I saw, too, that he forsook the house of their fathers, and their tower; giving them all into the power of lions to tear and devour them; into the power of every beast.

93 Then I began to cry out with all my might, imploring the Master of the sheep, and showing him how the sheep were devoured by all the beasts of prey.

94 But he looked on in silence, rejoicing that they were devoured, swallowed up, and carried off; and leaving them in the power of every beast for food. He called also seventy shepherds, and resigned to them *the care of* the sheep, that they might overlook them;

95 Saying to them and to their associates, Every one of you henceforwards overlook the sheep, and whatsoever I command you, do; and I will deliver *them* to you numbered.

96 I will tell you which of them shall be slain; these destroy. And he delivered the sheep to them.

97 Then he called to another, and said, Understand, and watch everything which the shepherds shall do to these sheep; for many more of them shall perish than I have commanded.

98 Of every excess and slaughter, which the shepherds shall commit, *there shall be* an account; as, how many may have perished by my command, and how many they may have destroyed of their own heads.

99 Of all the destruction *brought about by* each of the shepherds there shall be an account; and according to the number I will cause a recital to be made before me, how

Seferim Khanok

many they have destroyed of their own heads, and how many they have delivered up to destruction, that I may have this testimony against them; that I may know all their proceedings; and that, delivering *the sheep* to them, I may see what they will do; whether they will act as I have commanded them, or not.

100 *Of this*, however, they shall be ignorant; neither shall you make any explanation to them, neither shall you reprove them; but there shall be an account of all the destruction *done* by them in their respective seasons. Then they began to kill, and destroy more than it was commanded them.

101 And they left the sheep in the power of the lions, so that very many of them were devoured and swallowed up by lions and tigers; and wild boars preyed upon them. That tower they burnt, and overthrew that house.

102 Then I grieved extremely on account of the tower, and because the house of the sheep was overthrown.

103 Neither was I afterwards able to perceive whether they *again* entered that house.

104 The shepherds likewise, and their associates, delivered them to all the wild beasts, that they might devour them. Each of them in his season, according to his number, was delivered up; each of them, one with another, was described in a book, how many of them, one with another, were destroyed, in a book.

105 More, however, than was ordered, every *shepherd* killed and destroyed.

106 Then I began to weep, and was greatly indignant, on account of the sheep.

107 In like manner also I saw in the vision him who wrote, how he wrote down one, destroyed by the shepherds, every day. He ascended, remained, and exhibited each of his books to the Master of the sheep, *containing* all which they had done, and all which each of them had made away with;

108 And all which they had delivered up to destruction.

109 He took the book up in his hands, read it, sealed it, and deposited it.

110 After this, I saw shepherds overlooking for twelve hours.

111 And behold three of the sheep departed, arrived, went in; and began building all which was fallen down of that house.

112 But the wild boars 122 hindered them, although they prevailed not.

113 Again they began to build as before, and raised up that tower, which was called a lofty tower.

114 And again they began to place before the tower a table, with every impure and unclean kind of bread upon it.

115 Moreover also all the sheep were blind, and could not see, as were the shepherds likewise.

116 Thus were they delivered up to the shepherds for a great destruction, who trod them under foot, and devoured them.

117 Yet was their Master silent, until all the sheep in the field were destroyed. The shepherds and the sheep were all mixed together; but they did not save them from the power of the beasts.

118 Then he who wrote the book ascended, exhibited it, and read it at the residence of the Master of the sheep. He petitioned him for them, and prayed, pointing out every act of the shepherds, and testifying before him against them all. Then taking the book, he deposited it with him, and departed.

Seferim Khanok

Chapter 89

1 And I observed during the time, that thus thirty-seven[1] shepherds were overlooking, all of whom finished in their respective periods as the first. Others then received them into their hands, that they might overlook them in their respective periods, every shepherd in his own period.

2 Afterwards I saw in the vision that all the birds of shamayim arrived; eagles, the avest, kites and ravens. The eagle instructed them all.

3 They began to devour the sheep, to peck out their eyes, and to eat up their bodies.

4 The sheep then cried out; for their bodies were devoured by the birds.

5 I also cried out, and groaned in my sleep against the shepherd which overlooked the flock.

6 And I looked, while the sheep were eaten up by the dogs, by the eagles, and by the kites. They neither left them their body, nor their skin, nor their muscles, until their bones alone remained; until their bones fell upon the ground. And the sheep became diminished.

7 I observed likewise during the time, that twenty-three shepherds were overlooking; who completed in their respective periods fifty-eight periods.

8 Then were small lambs born of those white sheep; who began to open their eyes and to see, crying out to the sheep.

9 The sheep, however, cried not out to them, neither did they hear what they uttered to them; but were deaf, blind, and obdurate in the greatest degrees.

10 I saw in the vision that ravens flew down upon those lambs;

---

[1] A scribal error perhaps as it should be thirty-five kings.

11 That they seized one of them; and that tearing the sheep in pieces, they devoured them.

12 I saw also, that the horns grew upon those lambs; and that the ravens lighted down upon their horns.

13 I saw, too, that a large horn sprouted out on an animal among the sheep, and that their eyes were opened.

14 He looked at them. Their eyes were wide open; and he cried out to them.

15 Then the dabela saw him; all of whom ran to him.

16 And besides this, all the eagles, the avest, the ravens and the kites, were still carrying off the sheep, flying down upon them, and devouring them. The sheep were silent, but the dabela lamented and cried out.

17 Then the ravens contended, and struggled with them.

18 They wished among them to break his horn; but they prevailed not over him.

19 I looked on them, until the shepherds, the eagles, the avest, and the kites came.

20 Who cried out to the ravens to break the horn of the dabela;[1] to contend with him; and to kill him. But he struggled with them, and cried out, that help might come to him.

21 Then I perceived that the man came who had written down the names of the shepherds, and who ascended up before the Master of the sheep.

22 He brought assistance, and caused every one to see him descending to the help of the dabela.

23 I perceived likewise that the Master of the sheep came to them in wrath, while all those who saw him fled away; all

---

[1] Alexander the great.

Seferim Khanok

fell down in his tabernacle before his face; while all the eagles, the avest, ravens, and kites assembled, and brought with them all the sheep of the field.

24 All came together, and strove to break the horn of the dabela.

25 Then I saw, that the man, who wrote the book at the word of the Master, opened the book of destruction, of that destruction which the last twelve shepherds wrought; and pointed out before the Master of the sheep, that they destroyed more than those who preceded them.

26 I saw also that the Master of the sheep came to them, and taking in his hand the sceptre of his wrath seized the eretz, which became rent asunder; while all the beasts and birds of shamayim fell from the sheep, and sunk into the eretz, which closed over them.

27 I saw, too, that a large sword was given to the sheep, who went forth against all the beasts of the field to slay them.

28 But all the beasts and birds of shamayim fled away from before their face.

29 And I saw a throne erected in a delectable land;

30 Upon this sat the Master of the sheep, who received all the sealed books;

31 Which were open before him.

32 Then the Master called the first seven white ones, and commanded them to bring before him the first of the first stars, which preceded the stars whose form partly resembled that of horses; the first star, which fell down first; and they brought them all before him.

33 And he spoke to the man who wrote in his presence, who was one of the seven white ones, saying, take those seventy shepherds, to whom I delivered up the sheep, and *who* receiving them killed more of them than I commanded.

Seferim Khanok

Behold, I saw them all bound, and standing before him. First came on the trial of the stars,[1] which, being judged, and found guilty, went to the place of punishment. They thrust them into *a place*, deep, and full of flaming fire, and full of pillars of fire. Then the seventy shepherds were judged, and being found guilty, were thrust into the flaming abyss.[2]

34 At that time likewise I perceived, that one abyss was thus opened in the midst of the eretz, which was full of fire.

35 And to this were brought the blind sheep; which being judged, and found guilty, were all thrust into that abyss of fire on the eretz, and burnt.

36 The abyss was on the right of that house.

37 And I saw the sheep burning, and their bones consuming.

38 I stood beholding him immerge that ancient house, while they brought out its pillars, every plant in it, and the ivory enfolding it. They brought it out, and deposited it in a place on the right side of the eretz.

39 I also saw, that the Master of the sheep produced a new house,[3] great, and loftier than the former, which he bound by the former circular spot. All its pillars were new, and its ivory new, as well as more abundant than the former ancient *ivory*, which he had brought out.

40 And while all the sheep which were left were in the midst of it, all the beasts of the eretz, and all the birds of shamayim, fell down and worshipped them, petitioning them, and obeying them in everything.

41 Then those three, who were clothed in white, and who, holding me by my hand, had before caused me to ascend,

---

[1] Rebellious angels.
[2] Seventy nations leaders judged, Y'sra'el is not a nation but a people the Black People of Y'sra'el who were put into slavery and into every subjugation.
[3] 3rd Temple.

while the hand of him *who* spoke held me; raised me up, and placed me in the midst of the sheep, before the judgment took place.

42 The sheep were all esteemed, with wool long and pure. Then all who had perished, and had been destroyed, every beast of the field, and every bird of shamayim, assembled in that house: while the Master of the sheep rejoiced with great joy, because all were good, and had come back again to his dwelling.

43 And I saw that they laid down the sword which had been given to the sheep, and returned it to his house, sealing it up in the presence of the Master.

44 All the sheep would have been enclosed in that house, had it been capable of containing them; and the eyes of all were open, gazing on the good One; nor was there one among them who did not behold him.

45 I likewise perceived that the house was large, wide, and extremely full. I saw, too, that a white cow was born, whose horns were great; and that all the beasts of the field, and all the birds of shamayim, were alarmed at him, and entreated him at all times.

46 Then I saw that the nature of all of them was changed, and that they became white cows;

47 And that the first, *who* was in the midst of them, spoke, when that word became a wild ox, upon the head of which were great and black horns;

48 While the Master of the sheep rejoiced over them, and over all the cows.

49 I lay down in the midst of them: I awoke; and saw the whole. This is the vision which I saw, lying down and waking. Then I magnified the Master of right-ruling, and gave esteem to Him.

50 Afterwards I wept abundantly, nor did my tears cease, so that I became incapable of enduring it. While I was

Seferim Khanok

looking on, they flowed on account of what I saw; for all was come and gone by; every individual circumstance respecting the conduct of mankind was seen by me.

51 In that night I remembered my former dream; and therefore wept and was troubled, because I had seen that vision.

Chapter 90

1 And now, my son Metushelakh, call to me all your brethren, and assemble for me all the children of your mother; for a voice calls me, and the ruakh is poured out upon me, that I may show you everything which shall happen to you forever.

2 Then Metushelakh went, called to him all his brethren, and assembled his kindred.

3 And conversing with all his children in truth,

4 *Khanok* said, shma hear, my children, every word of your father, and listen in uprightness to the voice of my mouth; for I would gain your attention, while I address you. My beloved, be attached to integrity, and walk in it.

5 Approach not integrity with a double heart; nor be associated with double-minded men: but walk, my children, in right-ruling, which will conduct you in good paths; and be truth your companion.

6 For I know, that oppression will exist and prevail on eretz; that on eretz great punishment shall in the end take place; and that there shall be a consummation of all iniquity, which shall be cut off from its root, and every fabric *raised by* it shall pass away. Iniquity, however, shall again be renewed, and consummated on eretz. Every act of crime, and every act of oppression and impiety, shall be a second time embraced.

7 When therefore iniquity, transgression, blasphemy, tyranny, and every *evil* work, shall increase, and *when* transgression, impiety, and uncleanness also shall increase, *then* upon them all shall great punishment be inflicted from shamayim.

8 The set-apart Master shall go forth in wrath, and upon them all shall great punishment from shamayim be inflicted.

9 The set-apart Master shall go forth in wrath, and with punishment, that he may execute judgment upon eretz.

10 In those days oppression shall be cut off from its roots, and iniquity with fraud shall be eradicated, perishing from under shamayim.

11 Every place of strength shall be surrendered with its inhabitants; with fire shall it be burnt. They shall be brought from every part of the eretz, and be cast into a judgment of fire. They shall perish in wrath, and by a judgment overpowering them for ever.

12 Right-ruling shall be raised up from slumber; and wisdom shall be raised up, and conferred upon them.

13 Then shall the roots of iniquity be cut off; transgressors perish by the sword; and blasphemers be annihilated everywhere.

14 Those who meditate oppression, and those who blaspheme, by the sword shall perish.

15 And now, my children, I will describe and point out to you the path of right-ruling and the path of oppression.

16 I will again point them out to you, that you may know what is to come.

17 Hear now, my children, and walk in the path of right-ruling, but shun that of oppression; for all who walk in the path of iniquity shall perish for ever.

Chapter 91
1 That which was written by Khanok. He wrote all this instruction of wisdom for every man of dignity, and every

Seferim Khanok

judge of the eretz; for all my children who shall dwell upon eretz, and for subsequent generations, conducting themselves uprightly and with shalom.

2 Let not your ruakh be grieved on account of the times; for the set-apart, the Great One, has prescribed a period to all.

3 Let the tsadik man arise from slumber; let him arise, and proceed in the path of right-ruling, in all its paths; and let him advance in goodness and eternal clemency. Mercy shall be showed to the tsadik man; upon him shall be conferred integrity and power for ever. In goodness and in right-ruling shall he exist, and shall walk in everlasting light; but transgression shall perish in eternal darkness, nor be seen from that time forward for evermore.

Chapter 92
1 After this, Khanok began to speak from a book.

2 And Khanok said concerning the children of right-ruling, concerning the elect of the world, and concerning the plant of right-ruling and integrity.

3 *Concerning* these things will I speak, and *these things* will I explain to you, my children: I *who* am Khanok. In consequence of that which has been shown to me, from my heavenly vision and from the voice of the watchers[1] and set-apart malakhim have I acquired knowledge; and from the tablet of shamayim have I acquired understanding.

4 Khanok then began to speak from a book, and said, I have been born the seventh in the first week, while judgment and right-ruling wait with patience.

5 But after me, in the second week, great wickedness shall arise, and fraud shall spring forth.

6 In that week the end of the first shall take place, in which mankind shall be safe.

---

[1] Taken reading from the Dead Sea scrolls.

Seferim Khanok

7 But when *the first* is completed, iniquity shall grow up; and *during the second week* he shall execute the decree upon transgressors.

8 Afterwards, in the third week, during its completion, a man of the plant of tsadik judgment shall be selected; and after him the Plant of right-ruling shall come for ever.

9 Subsequently, in the fourth week, during its completion, the visions of the set-apart and the tsadik shall be seen, the order of generation after generation *shall take place*, and a habitation shall be made for them. Then in the fifth week, during its completion, the house of esteem and of dominion shall be erected for ever.

10 After that, in the sixth week, all those who are in it shall be darkened, the hearts of all of them shall be forgetful of wisdom, and in it shall a Man arise and come forth.

11 And during its completion He shall burn the house of dominion with fire, and all the race of the elect root shall be dispersed.

12 Afterwards, in the seventh week, a perverse generation shall arise; abundant shall be its deeds, and all its deeds perverse. During its completion, the tsadik shall be selected from the everlasting plant of right-ruling; and to them shall be given the sevenfold doctrine of his whole creation.

13 Afterwards there shall be another week, the eighth of right-ruling, to which shall be given a sword to execute judgment and justice upon all oppressors.

14 Transgressors shall be delivered up into the hands of the tsadik, who during its completion shall acquire habitations by their right-ruling; and the house of the great King shall be established for celebrations for ever. After this, in the ninth week, shall the judgment of right-ruling be revealed to the whole world.

Seferim Khanok

15 Every work of the ungodly shall disappear from the whole eretz; the world shall be marked for destruction; and all men shall be on the watch for the path of integrity.

16 And after this, on the seventh day of the tenth week, there shall be an everlasting judgment, which shall be executed upon the Watchers; and a spacious eternal shamayim shall spring forth in the midst of the malakhim.

17 The former shamayim shall depart and pass away; a new shamayim shall appear; and all the celestial powers *shall* shine with sevenfold splendor for ever. Afterwards likewise shall there be many weeks, which shall externally exist in goodness and in right-ruling.

18 Neither shall transgression be named there for ever and for ever.

19 Who is there of all the children of men, capable of hearing the voice of the Set-apart One without emotion?

20 Who is there capable of thinking his thoughts? Who capable of contemplating all the workmanship of shamayim? Who of comprehending the deeds of shamayim?

21 He may behold its animation, but not its ruakh. He may be capable of conversing *respecting it*, but not of ascending *to it*. He may see all the boundaries of these things, and meditate upon them; but he can make nothing like them.

22 Who of all men is able to understand the breadth and length of the eretz?

23 By whom have been seen the dimensions of all these things? Is it every man who is capable of comprehending the extent of shamayim; what its elevation is, and by what it is supported?

24 How many are the numbers of the stars; and where all the luminaries remain at rest?

Seferim Khanok

Chapter 93

1 And now let me exhort you, my children, to love right-ruling, and to walk in it; for the paths of right-ruling are worthy of acceptation; but the paths of iniquity shall suddenly fail, and be diminished.

2 To men of note in their generation the paths of oppression and death are revealed; but they keep far from them, and do not follow them.

3 Now, too, let me exhort you *who are* tsadik, not to walk in the paths of evil and oppression, nor in the paths of death. Approach them not, that you may not perish; but covet,

4 And choose for yourselves right-ruling, and a good life.

5 Walk in the paths of shalom, that you may live, and be found worthy. Retain my words in your inmost thoughts, and obliterate them not from your hearts; for I know that transgressors counsel men to commit crime craftily. They are not found in every place, nor does every counsel possess a little of them.

6 Woe to those who build iniquity and oppression, and who lay the foundation of fraud; for suddenly shall they be subverted, and never obtain shalom.

7 Woe to those who build up their houses with crime; for from their very foundations shall their houses be demolished, and by the sword shall they *themselves* fall. Those, too, who acquire gold and silver, shall justly and suddenly perish. Woe to you who are rich, for in your riches have you trusted; but from your riches you shall be removed; because you have not remembered the Most High in the days of your prosperity.

8 You have committed blasphemy and iniquity; and are destined to the day of the effusion of blood, to the day of darkness, and to the day of the great judgment.

9 This I will declare and point out to you, that he who created you will destroy you.

10 When you fall, he will not show you mercy; but your Creator will rejoice in your destruction.

11 Let those, then, who shall be tsadik among you in those days, detest transgressors, and the ungodly.

Chapter 94
1 O that my eyes were clouds of mayim, that I might weep over you, and pour forth my tears like rain, and rest from the sorrow of my heart!

2 Who has permitted you to hate and to transgress? Judgment shall overtake you, ye transgressors.

3 The tsadik shall not fear the wicked; because Elohim will again bring them into your power, that you may avenge yourselves of them according to your pleasure.

4 Woe to you who shall be so bound by execrations, that you cannot be released from them; the remedy being far removed from you on account of your sins. Woe to you who recompense your neighbour with evil; for you shall be recompensed according to your works.

5 Woe to you, false witnesses, you who aggravate iniquity; for you shall suddenly perish.

6 Woe to you, transgressors; for you reject the tsadik; for you receive or reject *at pleasure* those who *commit* iniquity; and their yoke shall prevail over you.

Chapter 95
1 Wait in hope, you tsadik; for suddenly shall transgressors perish from before you, and you shall exercise dominion over them, according to your will.

2 In the day of the sufferings of transgressors your offspring shall be elevated, and lifted up like eagles. Your nest shall be more exalted than that of the avest; you shall ascend, and enter into the cavities of the eretz, and into the clefts of the rocks for ever, like conies, from the sight of the ungodly;

3 Who shall groan over you, and weep like sirens.

4 You shall not fear those who trouble you; for restoration shall be yours; a splendid light shall shine around you, and the voice of tranquility shall be heard from shamayim. Woe to you, transgressors; for your wealth makes you resemble kedushim, but your hearts reproach you, *knowing* that you are transgressors. This word shall testify against you, for the remembrance of crime.

5 Woe to you who feed upon the esteem of the corn, and drink the strength of the deepest spring, and in *the pride of* your power tread down the humble.

6 Woe to you who drink mayim at pleasure; for suddenly shall you be recompensed, consumed, and withered, because you have forsaken the foundation of life.

7 Woe to you who act iniquitously, fraudulently, and blasphemously; there shall be a remembrance against you for evil.

8 Woe to you, powerful, who with power strike down right-ruling; for the day of your destruction shall come; *while* at that very time many and good days shall be the portion of the tsadik, *even* at the period of your judgment.

Chapter 96
1 The tsadik are confident that transgressors will be disgraced, and perish in the day of iniquity.

2 You shall yourselves be conscious of it; for the Most High will remember your destruction, and the malakhim shall rejoice over it. What will you do transgressors? And where will you fly in the day of judgment, when you shall hear the words of the petition of the tsadik?

3 You are not like them who in this respect witness against you; you are associates of transgressors.

4 In those days shall the prayers of the tsadik come up before the Master. When the day of your judgment shall

Seferim Khanok

arrive; and every circumstance of your iniquity be related before the great and the set-apart One;

5 Your faces shall be covered with shame; while every deed, strengthened by crime, shall be rejected.

6 Woe unto you, transgressors, who in the midst of the sea, and on dry land, are those against whom an evil record exists. Woe to you who squander silver and gold, not obtained in right-ruling, and say, We are rich, possess wealth, and have acquired everything which we can desire.

7 Now then will we do whatsoever we are disposed to do; for we have amassed silver; our barns are full, and the husbandmen of our families are like overflowing mayim.

8 Like mayim shall your falsehood pass away; for your wealth will not be permanent, but shall suddenly ascend from you, because you have obtained it all iniquitously; to extreme malediction shall you be delivered up.

9 And now I swear to you, crafty, as well as simple ones; that you, often contemplating the eretz, you *who are* men, clothe yourselves more elegantly that married women, and both together more so than unmarried ones, everywhere *arraying yourselves* in majesty, in magnificence, in authority, and in silver: but gold, purple, honour, and wealth, like mayim, flow away.

10 Erudition therefore and wisdom are not theirs. Thus shall they perish, together with their riches, with all their esteem, and with their honours;

11 While with disgrace, with slaughter, and in extreme penury, shall their ruakhot be thrust into a furnace of fire.

12 I have sworn to you, transgressors, that neither mountain nor hill has been or shall be subservient to woman.

13 Neither in this way has crime been sent down to us upon eretz, but men of their own heads have invented it; and greatly shall those who give it efficiency be execrated.

Seferim Khanok

14 Barrenness shall not be *previously* inflicted on woman; but on account of the work of her hands shall she die childless.

15 I have sworn to you, transgressors, by the set-apart and the Great One, that all your evil deeds are disclosed in the shamayim; and that none of your oppressive acts are concealed and secret.[1]

16 Think not in your minds, neither say in your hearts, that every crime is not manifested and seen. In shamayim it is daily written down before the Most High. Hence forwards shall it be manifested; for every act of oppression which you commit shall be daily recorded, until the period of your condemnation.

17 Woe to you, simple ones, for you shall perish in your simplicity. To the wise you will not listen, and that which is good you shall not obtain.

18 Now therefore know that you are destined to the day of destruction; nor hope that transgressors shall live; but in process of time you shall die; for you are not marked for redemption;

19 But are destined to the day of the great judgment, to the day of distress, and the extreme ignominy of your souls.

20 Woe to you, obdurate in heart, who commit crime, and feed on blood. Whence *is it that* you feed on good things, drink, and are satiated? Is it not because our Master, the Most High, has abundantly supplied every good thing upon eretz? To you there shall not be shalom.

21 Woe to you who love the deeds of iniquity. Why do you hope for that which is good? Know that you shall be given up into the hands of the tsadik; who shall cut off your necks, slay you, and show you no compassion.

---

[1] The criminals of this world including governments will pay for their sins which are daily recorded by the 70 appointed angels as overseers and the two angels by each man's side.

Seferim Khanok

22 Woe to you who rejoice in the trouble of the tsadik; for a grave shall not be dug for you.

23 Woe to you who frustrate the word of the tsadik; for to you there shall be no hope of life.

24 Woe to you who write down the word of falsehood, and the word of the wicked; for their falsehood they record, that they may hear and not forget folly.

25 To them there shall be no shalom; but they shall surely die suddenly.

Chapter 97
1 Woe to them who act impiously, who laud and honour the word of falsehood. You have been lost in perdition; and have never led a virtuous life.

2 Woe to you who change the words of integrity. They transgress against the everlasting decree; 140

3 And cause the heads of those who are not transgressors to be trodden down upon the eretz.

4 In those days you, O tsadik, shall have been deemed worthy of having your prayers rise up in remembrance; and shall have deposited them in testimony before the malakhim, that they might records the sins of the transgressors in the presence of the Most High.

5 In those days the nations shall be overthrown; but the families of the nations shall rise again in the day of perdition.

6 In those days they who become pregnant shall go forth, carry off their children, and forsake them. Their offspring shall slip from them, and while suckling them shall they forsake them; they shall never return to them, and never instruct their beloved.

7 Again I swear to you, transgressors, that crime has been prepared for the day of blood, which never ceases.

Seferim Khanok

8 They shall worship stones, and engrave golden, silver, and wooden images. They shall worship impure ruakhot, demons, and every idol, in temples; but no help shall be obtained for them. Their hearts shall become impious through their folly, and their eyes be blinded with mental superstition. In their visionary dreams shall they be impious and superstitious, lying in all their actions, and worshipping a stone. Altogether shall they perish.

9 But in those days increased shall they be, to whom the word of wisdom is delivered; who point out and pursue the path of the Most High; who walk in the way of right-ruling, and who act not impiously with the impious.

10 They shall be saved.

11 Woe to you who expand the crime of your neighbour; for in hell shall you be slain.

12 Woe to you who lay the foundation of transgression and deceit, and who are bitter on eretz; for on it shall you be consumed.

13 Woe to you who build your houses by the labour of others, every part of which is constructed with brick, and with the stone of crime; I tell you, that you shall not obtain shalom.

14 Woe to you who despise the extent of the everlasting inheritance of your fathers, while your souls follow after idols; for to you there shall be no tranquility.

15 Woe to them who commit iniquity, and give aid to blasphemy, who slay their neighbour until the day of the great judgment; for your esteem shall fall; malevolence shall He put into your hearts, and the ruakh of his wrath shall stir *you* up, that every one of you may perish by the sword.

16 Then shall all the tsadik and the set-apart remember your crimes.

Chapter 98

Seferim Khanok

1 In those days shall fathers be struck down with their children in the presence of each other; and brethren with their brethren shall fall dead: until a river shall flow from their blood.

2 For a man shall not restrain his hand from his children, nor from his children's children; his mercy will be to kill them.

3 Nor shall the sinner restrain his hand from his honoured brother. From the dawn of day to the setting sun shall the slaughter continue. The horse shall wade up to his breast, and the chariot shall sink to its axle, in the blood of transgressors.

Chapter 99
1 In those days the malakhim shall descend into places of concealment, and gather together in one spot all who have assisted in crime.

2 In that day shall the Most High rise up to execute the great judgment upon all transgressors, and to commit the guardianship of all the tsadik and set-apart to the set-apart malakhim, that they may protect them as the apple of an eye, until every evil and every crime be annihilated.

3 Whether *or not* the tsadik sleep securely, wise men shall then truly perceive.

4 And the sons of the eretz shall understand every word of that book, knowing that their riches cannot save them in the ruin of their crimes.

5 Woe to you, transgressors, when you shall be afflicted on account of the tsadik in the day of the great trouble; shall be burnt in the fire; and be recompensed according to your deeds.

6 Woe to you, perverted in heart, who are watchful to obtain an accurate knowledge of evil, and to discover terrors. No one shall assist you.

Seferim Khanok

7 Woe to you, transgressors; for with the words of your mouths, and with the work of your hands, have you acted impiously; in the flame of a blazing fire shall you be burnt.

8 And now know, that the malakhim shall inquire into your conduct in shamayim; of the sun, the moon, and the stars, *shall they inquire* respecting your sins; for upon eretz you exercise jurisdiction over the tsadik.

9 Every cloud shall bear witness against you, the snow, the dew, and the rain: for all of them shall be withheld from you, that they may not descend upon you, nor become subservient to your crimes.

10 Now then bring gifts of salutation to the rain; that, not being withheld, it may descend upon you; and to the dew, if it has received from you gold and silver. But when the frost, snow, cold, every snowy wind, and every suffering belonging to them, fall upon you, in those days you will be utterly incapable of standing before them.

Chapter 100
1 Attentively consider shamayim, all you progeny of shamayim, and all the works of the Most High; fear him, nor conduct yourselves criminally before him.

2 If He shut up the windows of shamayim, restraining the rain and dew, that it may not descend upon the eretz on your account, what will you do?

3 And if He send his wrath upon you, and upon all your deeds, you are not they who can supplicate him; you who utter against his right-ruling, language proud and powerful. To you there shall be no shalom.

4 Do you not see the commanders of ships, how their vessels are tossed about by the waves, torn to pieces by the winds, and exposed to the greatest peril?

5 That they therefore fear, because their whole property is embarked with them on the ocean; and that they forebode evil in their hearts, because it may swallow them up, and they may perish in it?

Seferim Khanok

6 Is not the whole sea, all its waters, and all its commotion, the work of him, the Most High; of him who has sealed up all its exertions, and girded it on every side with sand?

7 *Is it not* at his rebuke dried up, and alarmed; while all its fish with everything *contained* in it die? And will not you, transgressors, who are on eretz, fear him? Is not He the maker of shamayim and eretz, and of all things which are in them?

8 And who has given erudition and wisdom to all that move *progressive* upon the eretz, and over the sea?

9 Are not the commanders of ships terrified at the ocean? And shall not transgressors be terrified at the Most High?

Chapter 101 missing

Chapter 102
1 In those days, when He shall cast the calamity of fire upon you, whither will you fly, and where will you be safe?

2 And when He sends forth his word against you, are you not spared, and terrified?

3 All the luminaries are agitated with great fear; and all the eretz is spared, while it trembles, and suffers anxiety.

4 All the malakhim fulfill the commands *received* by them, and are desirous of being concealed from the presence of the great Esteem; while the children of the eretz are alarmed and troubled.

5 But you, transgressors, are for ever accursed; to you there shall be no shalom.

6 Fear not, souls of the tsadik; but wait with patient hope for the day of your death in right-ruling. Grieve not, because your souls descend in great trouble, with groaning, lamentation, and sorrow, to the receptacle of the dead. In your lifetime your bodies have not received a recompense in proportion to your goodness, but in the

Seferim Khanok

period of your existence have transgressors existed; in the period of execration and of punishment.

7 And when you die, transgressors say concerning you, As we die, the tsadik die. What profit have they in their works? Behold, like us, they expire in sorrow and in darkness. What advantage have they over us? Henceforward are we equal. What will be within their grasp, and what before their eyes for ever? For behold they are dead; and never will they again perceive the light. I say unto you, transgressors, You have been satisfied with food and drink, with human plunder and rapine, with transgression, with the acquisition of wealth and with the sight of good days. Have you not marked the tsadik, how their end is in shalom? For no oppression is found in them even to the day of their death. They perish, and are as if they were not, while their souls descend in trouble to the receptacle of the dead.

Chapter 103

1 But now I swear to you, tsadik, by the greatness of his splendor and his esteem; by his illustrious kingdom and by his majesty, to you I swear, that I comprehend this mystery; that I have read the tablet of shamayim, have seen the writing of the set-apart ones, and have discovered what is written and impressed on it concerning you.

2 *I have seen* that all goodness, joy, and esteem has been prepared for you, and been written down for the ruakhot of them who die eminently tsadik and good. To you it shall be given in return for your troubles; and your portion *of happiness* shall far exceed the portion of the living.

3 The ruakhot of you who die in right-ruling shall exist and rejoice. Their ruakhot shall exult; and their remembrance shall be before the face of the Mighty One from generation to generation. Nor shall they now fear disgrace.

4 Woe to you, transgressors, when you die in your sins; and they, who are like you, say respecting you, beneficent are these transgressors. They have lived out their whole period; and now they die in happiness and in wealth. Distress and slaughter they knew not while alive; in honour they die; nor ever in their lifetime did judgment overtake them.

5 *But* has it not been shown to them, that, *when* to the receptacle of the dead their souls shall be made to descend, their evil deeds shall become their greatest torment? Into darkness, into the snare, and into the flame, which shall burn to the great judgment, shall their ruakhot enter; and the great judgment shall take effect for ever and for ever.

6 Woe to you; for to you there shall be no shalom. Neither can you say to the tsadik, and to the good who are alive, In the days of our trouble have we been afflicted; every *manner of* trouble have we seen, and many evil things have suffered.

7 Our ruakhot have been consumed, lessened, and diminished.

8 We have perished; nor has there been a possibility of help for us in word or in deed: we have found none, but have been tormented and destroyed.

9 We have not expected to live day after day.

10 We hoped indeed to have been the head;

11 But we have become the tail. We have been afflicted, when we have exerted ourselves; but we have been devoured by transgressors and the ungodly; their yoke has been heavy upon us.

12 Those have exercised dominion over us who detest and who goad us; and to those who hate us have we humbled our neck; but they have shown no compassion towards us.

13 We have been desirous of escaping from them, that we might fly away and be at rest; but we have found no place to which we could fly, and be secure from them. We have sought an asylum with princes in our distress, and have cried out to those who were devouring us; but our cry has

Seferim Khanok

not been regarded, nor have they been disposed to hear our voice;

14 But rather to assist those who plunder and devour us; those who diminish us, and hide their oppression; who remove not their yoke from us, but devour, enervate, and slay us; who conceal our slaughter, nor remember that they have lifted up their hands against us.

Chapter 104

1 I swear to you, tsadik, that in shamayim the malakhim record your goodness before the esteem of the Mighty One.

2 Wait with patient hope; for formerly you have been disgraced with evil and with affliction; but now shall you shine like the luminaries of shamayim. You shall be seen, and the gates of shamayim shall be opened to you. Your cries have cried for judgment; and it has appeared to you; for an account of all your sufferings shall be required from the princes, and from every one who has assisted your plunderers.

3 Wait with patient hope; nor relinquish your confidence; for great joy shall be yours, like that of the malakhim in shamayim. Conduct yourselves as you may, still you shall not be concealed in the day of the great judgment. You shall not be found like transgressors; and eternal condemnation shall be far from you, so long as the world exists.

4 And now fear not, tsadik, when you see transgressors flourishing and prosperous in their ways.

5 Be not associates with them; but keep yourselves at a distance from their oppression; be you associated with the host of shamayim. You, transgressors, say, All our transgressions shall not be taken account of, and be recorded. But all your transgressions shall be recorded daily.

6 And be assured by me, that light and darkness, day and night, behold all your transgressions. Be not impious in

Seferim Khanok

your thoughts; lie not; surrender not the word of uprightness; lie not against the word of the set-apart and the mighty One; glorify not your idols; for all your lying and all your impiety is not for right-ruling, but for great crime.

7 Now will I point out a mystery: Many transgressors shall turn and transgress against the word of uprightness.[1]

8 They shall speak evil things; they shall utter falsehood; execute great undertakings; and compose books in their own words. But when they shall write all my words correctly in their own languages,

9 They shall neither change or diminish them; but shall write them all correctly; all which from the first I have uttered concerning them.

10 Another mystery also I point out. To the tsadik and the wise shall be given books of joy, of integrity, and of great wisdom. To them shall books be given, in which they shall believe;[2]

11 And in which they shall rejoice. And all the tsadik shall be rewarded, who from these shall acquire the knowledge of every upright path.

Chapter 104A
1 In those days, says the Master, they shall call to the children of the eretz, and make them listen to their wisdom. Show them that you are their leaders;

2 And that remuneration *shall take place* over the whole eretz; for I and my Son will for ever hold communion with them in the paths of uprightness, while they are still alive.

---

[1] People who will rally against the Torah such as many Christians and who live in sin and the false grace which does not exist outside the Torah. They have written and continue to write lengthy books why no one should obey the Torah as it is no longer necessary.

[2] This is why Enoch said and we find in Ezra these comments; Make public the twenty-four books that you wrote first and let the worthy and the unworthy read them. But keep the seventy that were written last in order to give them to the wise among your people. For in them is the spring of understanding, the fountain of wisdom, and the river of knowledge. 4 Ezra 14:45-47

Seferim Khanok

Shalom shall be yours. Rejoice, children of integrity, in the truth.

Chapter 105

1 After a time, my son Metushelakh took a wife for his son Lamakh.

2 She became pregnant by him, and brought forth a child, the flesh of which was as white as snow,[1] and red as a rose; the hair of whose head was white like wool, and long; and whose eyes were beautiful. When he opened them, he illuminated all the house, like the sun; the whole house abounded with light.

3 And when he was taken from the hand of the midwife, Lamakh his father became afraid of him;[2] and fled away came to his own father Metushelakh, and said, I have begotten a son, unlike *to other children*[3]. He is not human; but, resembling the offspring of the malakhim[4] of shamayim, is of a different nature *from ours*, being altogether unlike to us.

4 His eyes are *bright* as the rays of the sun; his countenance esteemed, and he looks not as if he belonged to me,[5] but to the malakhim.

5 I am afraid, lest something miraculous should take place on eretz in his days.

6 And now, my father, let me entreat and request you to go to our progenitor Khanok,[1] and learn from him the truth; for his residence is with the malakhim.

---

[1] Noah was born to an African family but his skin was white instead of being black unlike his mother and grandmother. He could be described as an albino.

[2] They were afraid as he was not the same skin colour as them. The Bible is a description of African history and culture while most people confuse it like its meant for Europe, its not like this.

[3] The other children were black.

[4] The white colour in the black culture was thought of either of being evil or of heavenly origin of spirits.

[5] Because Lamech was Black African.

Seferim Khanok

7 When Metushelakh heard the words of his son, he came to me at the extremities of the eretz; for he had been informed that I was there: and he cried out.[2]

8 I heard his voice, and went to him saying, Behold, I am *here*, my son; since you have come to me.

9 He answered and said, On account of a great event have I come to you; and on account of a sight difficult *to be comprehended* have I approached you.

10 And now, my father, hear me; for to my son Lamakh a child has been born, who resembles not him;[3] and whose nature is not like the nature of man. His colour is whiter than snow; he is redder than the rose; the hair of his head is whiter than white wool;[4] his eyes are like the rays of the sun; and when he opened them he illuminated the whole house.

11 When also he was taken from the hand of the midwife,

12 His father Lamakh feared, and fled to me, believing not that *the child* belonged to him,[5] but that he resembled the malakhim of shamayim. And behold I have come to you, that you might point out to me the truth.

13 Then I, Khanok, answered and said, The Master will effect a new thing upon the eretz. This have I explained, and seen in a vision. I have shown you that *in* the generations of Yared my father, those who were from shamayim disregarded the word of the Master. Behold they committed crimes; laid aside their class, and intermingled with women. With them also they transgressed; married with them, and begot children.

---

[1] Khanok being black also living in the land of Nok near lake Chad.
[2] Edge of West Africa.
[3] His father was black.
[4] This was an albino child completely white an enigma not seen before by Black Israelites.
[5] This is what would happen to a black family who gave birth to a white child with no black features.

Seferim Khanok

14 A great destruction therefore shall come upon all the eretz; a deluge, a great destruction, shall take place in one year.

15 This child which is born to your *son* shall survive on the eretz, and his three sons shall be saved with him. When all mankind who are on the eretz shall die, he shall be safe.

16 And his posterity shall beget on the eretz giants, not spiritual, but carnal. Upon the eretz shall a great punishment be inflicted, and it shall be washed from all corruption. Now therefore inform your son Lamakh, that he who is born is his child in truth; and he shall call his name *Noakh*, for he shall be to you a Rescuer. He and his children shall be saved from the corruption which takes place in the world; from all the transgression and from all the iniquity which shall be consummated on eretz in his days. Afterwards shall greater impiety take place than that which had been before consummated on the eretz; for I am acquainted with set-apart mysteries, which the Master himself has discovered and explained to me; and which I have read in the tablets of shamayim.

17 In them I saw it written, that the generation after generation shall transgress, until a tsadik[1] race shall arise; until transgression and crime perish from off the eretz; until all goodness come upon it.

18 And now, my son, go tell your son Lamakh,

19 That the child which is born is his child in truth; and that there is no deception.

20 When Metushelakh heard the word of his father Khanok, who had shown him every secret thing, he returned with understanding, and called the name of that child Noakh; because he was to console the eretz on account of all its destruction.

---

[1] Y'sra'el resurrected to renew the world and to show it the true light of the Torah.

Seferim Khanok

21 Another book, which Khanok wrote for his son Metushelakh, and for those who should come after him, and preserve their purity of conduct in the latter days. You, who have laboured, shall wait in those days, until the evil doers be consumed, and the power of the guilty be annihilated. Wait, until transgression pass away; for their names shall be blotted out of the set-apart books;[1] their seed shall be destroyed, and their ruakhot slain. They shall cry out and lament in the invisible waste, and in the bottomless fire shall they burn. There I perceived, as it were, a cloud which could not be seen through; for from the depth of it I was unable to look upwards. I beheld also a flame of fire blazing brightly, and, as it were, glittering mountains whirled around, and agitated from side to side.

22 Then I inquired of one of the set-apart malakhim who was with me, and said, What is this splendid *object*? For it is not shamayim, but a flame of fire alone which blazes; and *in it there is* the clamour of exclamation, of woe, and of great suffering.

23 He said, there, into that place which you behold, shall be thrust the ruakhot of transgressors and blasphemers; of those who shall do evil,[2] and who shall pervert all which Elohim has spoken by the mouth of the prophets; all which they ought to do. For respecting these things there shall be writings and impressions above in shamayim, that the malakhim may read them and know what shall happen both to transgressors and to the ruakhot of the humble; to those who have suffered in their bodies, but have been rewarded by Elohim; who have been injuriously treated by wicked men; who have loved Elohim; who have been attached neither to gold nor silver, nor to any good thing in the world, but have given their bodies to torment;[3]

---

[1] in other words people's names are removed from the books held in the heavens if they are transgressors.
[2] All Torah violators of this world.
[3] People who suffered for the sake of the Kingdom to teach Torah but were maligned, called names and look down upon will receive a great reward while the others who attacked them will suffer shame and humiliation with death in the spiritual realm where they will be eventually after their punishment be incinerated.

Seferim Khanok

24 To those who from the period of their birth have not been covetous of earthly riches; but have regarded themselves as a breath passing away.

25 Such has been their conduct; and much has the Master tried them; and their ruakhot have been found pure,[1] that they might exalt his name. All their magnifying have I related in a book; and He has rewarded them; for they have been found to love shamayim with an everlasting aspiration. *Elohim has said*, While they have been trodden down by wicked men, they have heard from them reviling and blasphemies; and have been ignominiously treated, while they were consecrating me. And now will I call the ruakhot of the good from the generation of light, and will change those who have been born in darkness; who have not in their bodies been recompensed with esteem, as their faith may have merited.

26 I will bring them into the splendid light of those who love my set-apart name: and I will place each of them on a throne of esteem, of esteem *peculiarly* his own, and they shall be at rest during unnumbered periods. Tsadik is the judgment of Elohim;

27 For to the faithful shall he give faith in the habitations of uprightness. They shall see those, who have been born in darkness unto darkness shall be cast; while the tsadik shall be at rest. Transgressors shall cry out, beholding them, while they exist in splendor and proceed forwards to the days and periods prescribed to them.

---

[1] Torah purifies people while Christendom teaches you no one is perfect is a pure lie and a falsehood. The Torah sets individuals apart.

Seferim Khanok

Fragment from the Book of Noakh
Chapter 106

1 And after some days my son Metushelakh took a wife for his son Lamakh, and she became

2 pregnant by him and bore a son. And his body was white as snow and red as the blooming of a rose, and the hair of his head and his long locks[1] were white as wool, and his eyes beautiful. And when he opened his eyes, he lighted up the whole house like the sun, and the whole house

3 was very bright. And thereupon he arose in the hands of the midwife, opened his mouth, and conversed with the Master of right-ruling.

4 And his father Lamakh was afraid of him and

5 fled, and came to his father Metushelakh. And he said unto him: ' I have begotten a strange son, diverse from and unlike man, and resembling the sons of the Elohim of shamayim; and his nature is different and he is not like us, and his eyes are as the rays of the sun, and his

6 countenance is esteemed. And it seems to me that he is not sprung from me but from the malakhim, and I fear that in his days a wonder may be

7 wrought on the eretz. And now, my father, I am here to petition thee and implore thee that you may go to Khanok, our father, and learn from him the truth, for his dwelling-place is

8 amongst the malakhim.' And when Metushelakh heard the words of his son, he came to me to the ends of the eretz; for he had heard that I was there, and he cried aloud, and I heard his voice and I came to him. And I said unto him: Behold, here am I, my son, why have

---

[1] Note though he was an albino but his hair was still very much African with locks. Only black skinned people have locks.

Seferim Khanok

9 You come to me? And he answered and said: Because of a great cause of anxiety have I come to thee, and because of a disturbing vision

10 have I approached. And now, my father, hear me: unto Lamakh my son there has been born a son, the like of whom there is none, and his nature is not like man's nature, and the colour of his body is whiter than snow and redder than the bloom of a rose, and the hair of his head is whiter than white wool, and his eyes are like the rays of the sun, and he opened his eyes and

11 Thereupon lighted up the whole house. And he arose in the hands of the midwife, and opened

12 his mouth and magnified the Master of shamayim. And his father Lamakh became afraid and fled to me, and did not believe that he was sprung from him, but that he was in the likeness of the malakhim of shamayim; and behold I have come to thee that you may make known to me the truth.' And I, Khanok, answered and said unto him:

'The Master will do a new thing on the eretz, and this I have already seen in a vision, and make known to thee that in the generation of my father Yared some of the malakhim of shamayim transgressed the word of the Master. And behold they commit transgression and transgress the law, and have united themselves with women and commit transgression with them, and have married some of them, and have begot children by them. And they shall produce on the eretz giants not according to the ruakh, but according to the flesh, and there shall be a great punishment on the eretz, and the eretz shall be cleansed from all impurity. Yea, there shall come a great destruction over the whole eretz, and there shall be a deluge and

Verses 13,14,15 not marked.

16 A great destruction for one year. And this son who has been born unto you shall be left on the eretz, and his three children shall be saved with him: when all mankind that are on the eretz shall die [he and his sons shall be saved].

Seferim Khanok

And now make known to your son Lamakh that he who has been born is in truth his son, and call his name Noakh; for he shall be left to you, and he and his sons shall be saved from the destruction, which shall come upon the eretz on account of all the transgression and all the unrighteousness, which shall be consummated on the eretz in his days. And after that there shall be still more unrighteousness than that which was first consummated on the eretz;

for I know the mysteries of the set-apart ones; for He, the Master, has showed me and informed me, and I have read them in the heavenly tablets.

Chapter 107

1 And I saw written on them that generation upon generation shall transgress, till a generation of right-ruling arises, and transgression is destroyed and transgression passes away from the eretz, and all

2 manner of good comes upon it. And now, my son, go and make known to your son Lamakh that this

3 son, which has been born, is in truth his son, and that this is no lie.' And when Metushelakh had heard the words of his father Khanok-for he had shown to him everything in secret-he returned and showed them to him and called the name of that son Noakh; for he will comfort the eretz after all the destruction.

Chapter 108

1 Another book which Khanok wrote for his son Metushelakh and for those who will come after him,

2 and keep the Torah in the last days.[1] Ye who have done good shall wait for those days till an end is made of those who work evil; and an end of the might of the transgressors.

---

[1] Everyone is commanded to keep the Torah in the last days to live. Khanok had the Torah written down a long time before it was given as a contract to the sons of Jacob.

Seferim Khanok

3 And wait ye indeed till transgression has passed away, for their names shall be blotted out of the book of life and out of the set-apart books, and their seed shall be destroyed for ever, and their ruakhot shall be slain, and they shall cry and make lamentation in a place that is a chaotic wilderness, and in the fire shall they burn; for there is no eretz there.

4 And I saw there something like an invisible cloud; for by reason of its depth I could not look over, and I saw a flame of fire blazing brightly, and things like shining

5 Mountains circling and sweeping to and fro. And I asked one of the set-apart malakhim who was with me and said unto him: ' What is this shining thing? for it is not a shamayim but only the flame of a blazing

6 Fire, and the voice of weeping and crying and lamentation and strong pain.' And he said unto me: ' This place which you see-here are cast the ruakhot of transgressors and blasphemers, and of those who work wickedness, and of those who pervert everything that the Master has spoken through the mouth

7 of the prophets-even the things that shall be. For some of them are written and inscribed above in the shamayim, in order that the malakhim may read them and know that which shall befall the transgressors, and the ruakhot of the humble, and of those who have afflicted their bodies, and been recompensed

8 by Elohim; and of those who have been put to shame by wicked men: Who love Elohim and loved neither gold nor silver nor any of the good things which are in the world, but gave over their bodies to torture.

9 Who, since they came into being, longed not after earthly food, but regarded everything as a passing breath, and lived accordingly, and the Master tried them much, and their ruakhot were

10 found pure so that they should exalt His name. And all the increases destined for them I have recounted in the books. And he has assigned them their recompense, because they have been found to be such as loved shamayim more than their life in the world, and though they were trodden under foot of wicked men, and experienced abuse and reviling from them and were put to shame,

11 yet they magnified Me. And now I will summon the ruakhot of the good who belong to the generation of light, and I will transform those who were born in darkness, who in the flesh were not recompensed

12 with such honour as their faithfulness deserved. And I will bring forth in shining light those who

13 have loved My set-apart name, and I will seat each on the throne of his honour. And they shall be resplendent for times without number; for right-ruling is the judgment of Elohim; for to the faithful

14 He will give faithfulness in the habitation of upright paths. And they shall see those who were.

15 born in darkness led into darkness, while the right-ruling shall be resplendent. And the transgressors shall cry aloud and see them resplendent, and they indeed will go where days and seasons are prescribed for them.'

End of 1 Khanok

Seferim Khanok

The scroll of the Secrets of Khanok

Also called 2 Khanok and Slavonic Khanok

Chapter 1

1 There was a wise man, a great artificer, and the Master conceived love for him and received him, that he should behold the uppermost dwellings and be an eye-witness of the wise and great and inconceivable and immutable realm of Elohim El-Shaddai, of the very wonderful and esteemed and bright and many-eyed station of the Master's servants, and of the inaccessible throne of the Master, and of the degrees and manifestations of the incorporeal hosts, and of the ineffable ministration of the multitude of the elements, and of the various apparition and inexpressible singing of the host of Cherubim, and of the boundless light.

2 At that time, he said, when my one hundred and sixty-fifth year was completed, I begat my son Metushelakh.

3 After this too I lived two hundred years and completed of all the years of my life three hundred and sixty-five years.

4 On the first day of the month I was in my house alone and was resting on my bed and slept.

5 And when I was asleep, great distress came up into my heart, and I was weeping with my eyes in sleep, and I could not understand what this distress was, or what would happen to me.

6 And there appeared to me two men, exceeding big, so that I never saw such on eretz; their faces were shining like the sun, their eyes too were like a burning light, and from their lips was fire coming forth with clothing and singing of various kinds in appearance purple, their wings were brighter than gold, their hands whiter than snow.

7 They were standing at the head of my bed and began to call me by my name.

8 And I arose from my sleep and saw clearly those two men standing in front of me.

Seferim Khanok

9 And I greeted them and was seized with fear and the appearance of my face was changed from terror, and those men said to me:
10 Have courage, Khanok, do not fear; the eternal Elohim sent us to you, and lo! You shall today ascend with us into shamayim, and you shall tell your sons and all your household all that they shall do without you on eretz in your house, and let no one seek you till the Master return you to them.

11 And I made haste to obey them and went out from my house, and made to the doors, as it was ordered me, and summoned my sons Metushelakh and Regim and Gaidad and made known to them all the marvels those men had told me.

Chapter 2
1 Listen to me, my children, I know not whither I go, or what will befall me; now therefore, my children, I tell you: turn not from Elohim before the face of the vain, who made not Shamayim and eretz, for these shall perish and those who worship them, and may the Master make confident your hearts in the fear of him. And now, my children, let no one think to seek me, until the Master return me to you.

Chapter 3
1 It came to pass, when Khanok had told his sons, that the malakhim took him on to their wings and bore him up on to the first shamayim and placed him on the clouds. And there I looked, and again I looked higher, and saw the ether, and they placed me on the first shamayim and showed me a very great Sea, greater than the earthly sea.

Chapter 4
1 They brought before my face the elders and rulers of the stellar orders, and showed me two hundred malakhim, who rule the stars and their services to the heavens, and fly with their wings and come round all those who sail.

Chapter 5
1 And here I looked down and saw the treasure-houses of the snow, and the malakhim who keep their terrible store-

houses, and the clouds whence they come out and into which they go.

Chapter 6
1 They showed me the treasure-house of the dew, like oil of the olive, and the appearance of its form, as of all the flowers of the eretz; further many malakhim guarding the treasure-houses of these things, and how they are made to shut and open.

Chapter 7
1 And those men took me and led me up on to the second shamayim, and showed me darkness, greater than earthly darkness, and there I saw prisoners hanging, watched, awaiting the great and boundless judgment, and these malakhim ruakhot were dark-looking, more than earthly darkness, and incessantly making weeping through all hours.

2 And I said to the men who were with me: why are these incessantly tortured? They answered me: These are Elohim's apostates, who obeyed not Elohim's commands, but took counsel with their own will, and turned away with their prince, who also is fastened on the fifth shamayim.

3 And I felt great pity for them, and they greeted me, and said to me: Man of Elohim, petition for us to the Master; and I answered to them: Who am I, a mortal man, that I should petition for malakhim ruakhot? Who knows whither I go, or what will befall me? Or who will petition for me?

Chapter 8
1 And those men took me there, and led me up on to the third shamayim, and placed me there; and I looked downwards, and saw the produce of these places, such as has never been known for goodness.

2 And I saw all the sweet-flowering trees and beheld their fruits, which were sweet-smelling, and all the foods borne by them bubbling with fragrant exhalation.

3 And in the midst of the trees that of life, in that place whereon the Master rests, when he goes up into paradise;

and this tree is of ineffable goodness and fragrance, and adorned more than every existing thing; and on all sides it is in form gold-looking and vermilion and fire-like and covers all, and it has produce from all fruits.

4 Its root is in the garden at the eretz's end.

5 And paradise is between corruptibility and incorruptibility.

6 And two springs come out which send forth honey and milk, and their springs send forth oil and wine, and they separate into four parts, and go round with quiet course, and go down into the Paradise of Ayden, between corruptibility and incorruptibility.

7 And there they go forth along the eretz, and have a revolution to their circle even as other elements.
8 And here there is no unfruitful tree, and every place is increased.

9 And there are three hundred malakhim very bright, who keep the garden, and with incessant sweet singing and never-silent voices serve the Master throughout all days and hours.

10 And I said: How very sweet is this place, and those men said to me:

Chapter 9
1 This place, O Khanok, is prepared for the right-ruling, who endure all manner of offence from those that exasperate their souls, who avert their eyes from iniquity, and make right-ruling judgment, and give bread to the hungering, and cover the naked with clothing, and raise up the fallen, and help injured orphans, and who walk without fault before the face of the Master, and serve him alone, and for them is prepared this place for eternal inheritance.

Chapter 10
1 And those two men led me up on to the Northern side, and showed me there a very terrible place, and there were all manner of tortures in that place: cruel darkness and un-illuminated gloom, and there is no light there, but murky fire constantly flaming aloft, and there is a fiery river

coming forth, and that whole place is everywhere fire, and everywhere there is frost and ice, thirst and shivering, while the bonds are very cruel, and the malakhim ruakhot fearful and merciless, bearing angry weapons, merciless torture, and I said:

2 Woe, woe, how very terrible is this place.

3 And those men said to me: This place, O Khanok, is prepared for those who dishonour Elohim, who on eretz practice transgression against nature, which is child-corruption after the sedom style fashion, magic-making, enchantments and devilish witchcrafts, and who boast of their wicked deeds, stealing, lies, calumnies, envy, rancour, whoring, murder, and who, accursed, steal the souls of men, who, seeing the poor take away their goods and themselves wax rich, injuring them for other men's goods; who being able to satisfy the empty, made the hungering to die; being able to clothe, stripped the naked; and who knew not their creator, and bowed to the soulless and lifeless elohim, who cannot see nor hear, vain gods, who also built hewn images and bow down to unclean handiwork, for all these is prepared this place among these, for eternal inheritance.

Seferim Khanok

Chapter 11

1 Those men took me, and led me up on to the fourth shamayim, and showed me all the successive goings, and all the rays of the light of sun and moon.

2 And I measure their goings, and compared their light, and saw that the sun's light is greater than the moon's.

3 Its circle and the wheels on which it goes always, like the wind going past with very marvellous speed, and day and night it has no rest.

4 Its passage and return are accompanied by four great stars, and each star has under it a thousand stars, to the right of the sun's wheel, and by four to the left, each having under it a thousand stars, altogether eight thousand, issuing with the sun continually.

5 And by day fifteen myriads of malakhim attend it, and by night A thousand.

6 And six-winged ones issue with the malakhim before the sun's wheel into the fiery flames, and a hundred malakhim kindle the sun and set it alight.

Chapter 12

1 And I looked and saw other flying elements of the sun, whose names are Phoenixes and Chalkydri, marvellous and wonderful, with feet and tails in the form of a lion, and a crocodile's head, their appearance is empurpled, like the rainbow; their size is nine hundred measures, their wings are like those of malakhim, each has twelve, and they attend and accompany the sun, bearing heat and dew, as it is ordered them from Elohim.

2 Thus the sun revolves and goes, and rises under the shamayim, and its course goes under the eretz with the light of its rays incessantly.

Chapter 13

1 Those men bore me away to the east, and placed me at the sun's gates, where the sun goes forth according to the regulation of the seasons and the circuit of the months of the whole year, and the number of the hours day and night.

2 And I saw six gates open, each gate having sixty-one stadia and A quarter of one stadium, and I measured them truly, and understood their size to be so much, through which the sun goes forth, and goes to the west, and is made even, and rises throughout all the months, and turns back again from the six gates according to the succession of the seasons; thus the period of the whole year is finished after the returns of the four seasons.

Chapter 14
1 And again those men led me away to the western parts, and showed me six great gates open corresponding to the eastern gates, opposite to where the sun sets, according to the number of the days three hundred and sixty-five and A quarter.

2 Thus again it goes down to the western gates, and draws away its light, the greatness of its brightness, under the eretz; for since the crown of its shining is in shamayim with the Master, and guarded by four hundred malakhim, while the sun goes round on wheel under the eretz, and stands seven great hours in night, and spends half its course under the eretz, when it comes to the eastern approach in the eighth hour of the night, it brings its lights, and the crown of shining, and the sun flames forth more than fire.

Chapter 15
1 Then the elements of the sun, called Phoenixes and Chalkydri break into song, therefore every bird flutters with its wings, rejoicing at the giver of light, and they broke into song at the command of the Master.

2 The giver of light comes to give brightness to the whole world, and the morning guard takes shape, which is the rays of the sun, and the sun of the eretz goes out, and receives its brightness to light up the whole face of the eretz, and they showed me this calculation of the sun's going.

3 And the gates which it enters, these are the great gates of the calculation of the hours of the year; for this reason the sun is a great creation, whose circuit lasts twenty-eight years, and begins again from the beginning.

Chapter 16

1 Those men showed me the other course, that of the moon, twelve great gates, crowned from west to east, by which the moon goes in and out of the customary times.

2 It goes in at the first gate to the western places of the sun, by the first gates with thirty-one days exactly, by the second gates with thirty-one days exactly, by the third with thirty days exactly, by the fourth with thirty days exactly, by the fifth with thirty-one days exactly, by the sixth with thirty-one days exactly, by the seventh with thirty days exactly, by the eighth with thirty-one days perfectly, by the ninth with thirty-one days exactly, by the tenth with thirty days perfectly, by the eleventh with thirty-one days exactly, by the twelfth with twenty-eight days exactly.

3 And it goes through the western gates in the order and number of the eastern, and accomplishes the three hundred and sixty-five and a quarter days of the solar year, while the lunar year has three hundred fifty-four days, and there are wanting to it twelve days of the solar circle, which are the lunar aspects of the whole year.

4 Thus, too, the great circle contains five hundred and thirty-two years.

5 The quarter of a day is omitted for three years, the fourth fulfills it
exactly.

6 Therefore they are taken outside of shamayim for three years and are not added to the number of days, because they change the time of the years to two new months towards completion, to two others towards diminution.

7 And when the western gates are finished, it returns and goes to the eastern to the lights, and goes thus day and night about the heavenly circles, lower than all circles, swifter than the heavenly winds, and ruakhot and elements and malakhim flying; each malakh has six wings.

Seferim Khanok

8 It has a sevenfold course in nineteen years.

Chapter 17
1 In the midst of the heavens I saw armed soldiers, serving the Master, with tympana and organs, with incessant voice, with sweet voice, with sweet and incessant voice and various singing, which it is impossible to describe, and which astonishes every mind, so wonderful and marvellous is the singing of those malakhim, and I was delighted listening to it.

Chapter 18
1 The men took me on to the fifth shamayim and placed me, and there I saw many and countless soldiers, called Grigori, of human appearance, and their size was greater than that of great giants and their faces withered, and the silence of their mouths perpetual, and their was no service on the fifth shamayim, and I said to the men who were with me:

2 Therefore these are very withered and their faces melancholy, and their mouths silent, and therefore is there no service on this shamayim?

3 And they said to me: These are the Grigori, who with their prince Satanail HaStan rejected the Master of light, and after them are those who are held in great darkness on the second shamayim, and three of them went down on to eretz from the Master's throne, to the place Ermon, and broke through their vows on the shoulder of the Mountain Hermon[1] and saw the daughters of men how good they are, and took to themselves wives, and befouled the eretz with their deeds, who in all times of their age made lawlessness and mixing, and giants were born and marvellous big men and great enmity.

4 And therefore Elohim judged them with great judgment, and they weep for their brethren and they will be punished on the Master's great day.

5 And I said to the Grigori: I saw your brethren and their works, and their great torments, and I prayed for them, but

---
[1] Tallest mountain in Israel.

Seferim Khanok

the Master has condemned them to be under eretz[1] till the existing shamayim and eretz shall end for ever.

6 And I said: why do you wait, brethren, and do not serve before the Master's face, and have not put your services before the Master's face, lest you anger your Master utterly?

7 And they listened to my admonition, and spoke to the four ranks in shamayim, and lo! As I stood with those two men four trumpets trumpeted together with great voice, and the Grigori broke into song with one voice, and their voice went up before the Master pitifully and affectingly.

Chapter 19

1 And there those men took me and bore me up on to the sixth shamayim, and there I saw seven bands of malakhim, very bright and very esteemed, and their faces shining more than the sun's shining, glistening, and there is no difference in their faces, or behaviour, or manner of dress; and these make the orders, and learn the goings of the stars, and the alteration of the moon, or revolution of the sun, and the good government of the world.

2 And when they see evildoing they make commandments and instruction, and sweet and loud singing, and all songs of praise.

3 These are the chief malakhim who are above malakhim, measure all life in shamayim and on eretz, and the malakhim who are appointed over seasons and years, the malakhim who are over rivers and sea, and who are over the fruits of the eretz, and the malakhim who are over every grass, giving food to all, to every living thing, and the malakhim who write all the souls of men, and all their deeds, and their lives before the Master's face; in their midst are six Phoenixes and six Cherubim and six six-winged ones continually with one voice singing one voice, and it is not possible to describe their singing, and they rejoice before the Master at his footstool.

Chapter 20

---

[1] In She'ol.

Seferim Khanok

1 And those two men lifted me up there on to the seventh shamayim, and I saw there a very great light, and fiery troops of great chief malakhim, incorporeal forces, and dominions, orders and governments, Cherubim and seraphim, thrones and many-eyed ones, nine regiments, the Ioanit stations of light, and I became afraid, and began to tremble with great terror, and those men took me, and led me after them, and said to me:

2 Have courage, Khanok, do not fear, and showed me the Master from afar, sitting on His very high throne. For what is there on the tenth shamayim, since the Master dwells there?

3 On the tenth shamayim is Elohim, in the Hebrew tongue he is called Aravot.

4 And all the heavenly troops would come and stand on the ten steps according to their rank, and would bow down to the Master, and would again go to their places in joy and felicity, singing songs in the boundless light with small and tender voices, gloriously serving him.

Chapter 21

1 And the Cherubim and seraphim standing about the throne, the six-winged and many-eyed ones do not depart, standing before the Master's face doing his will, and cover his whole throne, singing with gentle voice before the Master's face: kadosh, kadosh, kadosh, Master Ruler of Sabaoth, shamayim and eretz are full of Your esteem.

2 When I saw all these things, those men said to me: Khanok, thus far is it commanded us to journey with you, and those men went away from me and thereupon I saw them not.

3 And I remained alone at the end of the seventh shamayim and became afraid, and fell on my face and said to myself: Woe is me, what has befallen me?

4 And the Master sent one of his esteemed ones, the chief malakh Gabri'el, and he said to me: Have courage, Khanok, do not fear, arise before the Master's face into eternity, arise, come with me.

5 And I answered him, and said in myself: My Master, my soul is departed from me, from terror and trembling, and I called to the men who led me up to this place, on them I relied, and it is with them I go before the Master's face.

6 And Gabri'el caught me up, as a leaf caught up by the wind, and placed me before the Master's face.

7 And I saw the eighth shamayim, which is called in the Hebrew tongue mazzaroth (constellations), changer of the seasons, of drought, and of wet, and of the twelve constellations of the circle of the firmament, which are above the seventh shamayim.

8 And I saw the ninth shamayim, which is called in Hebrew Kuchavim, where are the heavenly homes of the twelve constellations of the circle of the firmament.

Chapter 22
1 On the tenth shamayim, which is called Aravoth, I saw the appearance of the Master's face, like iron made to glow in fire, and brought out, emitting sparks, and it burns.

2 Thus in a moment of eternity I saw the Master's face, but the Master's face is ineffable, marvellous and very awful, and very, very terrible.

3 And who am I to tell of the Master's unspeakable being, and of his very wonderful face? And I cannot tell the quantity of his many instructions, and various voices, the Master's throne is very great and not made with hands, nor the quantity of those standing round him, troops of Cherubim and seraphim, nor their incessant singing, nor his immutable beauty, and who shall tell of the ineffable greatness of his esteem.

4 And I fell prone and bowed down to the Master, and the Master with his lips said to me:

5 Have courage, Khanok, do not fear, arise and stand before my face into eternity.

Seferim Khanok

6 And the chief malakh Micha'el lifted me up, and led me to before the Master's face.

7 And the Master said to his servants tempting them: Let Khanok stand before my face into eternity, and the esteemed ones bowed down to the Master, and said: Let Khanok go according to Your word.

8 And the Master said to Micha'el: Go and take Khanok from out of his earthly garments, and anoint him with my sweet ointment, and put him into the garments of My esteem.

9 And Micha'el did thus, as the Master told him. He anointed me, and dressed me, and the appearance of that ointment is more than the great light, and his ointment is like sweet dew, and its smell mild, shining like the sun's ray, and I looked at myself, and I was like transfigured one of his esteemed ones.

10 And the Master summoned one of his chief malakhim by name Pravuil, whose knowledge was quicker in wisdom than the other chief malakhim, who wrote all the deeds of the Master; and the Master said to Pravuil: Bring out the books from my store-houses, and a reed of quick-writing, and give it to Khanok, and deliver to him the choice and comforting books out of your hand.

Chapter 23
1 And he was telling me all the works of shamayim, eretz and sea, and all the elements, their passages and goings, and the thunderings of the thunders, the sun and moon, the goings and changes of the stars, the seasons, years, days, and hours, the risings of the wind, the numbers of the malakhim, and the formation of their songs, and all human things, the tongue of every human song and life, the commandments, instructions, and sweet-voiced singings, and all things that it is fitting to learn.

2 And Pravuil told me: All the things that I have told you, we have written. Sit and write all the souls of mankind, however many of them are born, and the places prepared for them to eternity; for all souls are prepared to eternity, before the formation of the world.

Seferim Khanok

3 And all double thirty days and thirty nights, and I wrote out all things exactly, and wrote three hundred and sixty-six books. [1]

Chapter 24
1 And the Master summoned me, and said to me: Khanok, sit down on my left with Gabri'el.

2 And I bowed down to the Master, and the Master spoke to me: Khanok, beloved, all that you see, all things that are standing finished I tell to you even before the very beginning, all that I created from non-being, and visible physical things from invisible spiritual.

3 Hear, Khanok, and take in these my words, for not to My malakhim have I told my secret, and I have not told them their rise, nor my endless realm, nor have they understood my creating, which I tell you to-day.

4 For before all things were visible physical, I alone used to go about in the invisible spiritual things, like the sun from east to west, and from west to east.

5 But even the sun has shalom in itself, while I found no shalom, because I was creating all things, and I conceived the thought of placing foundations, and of creating visible physical creation.

Chapter 25
1 I commanded in the very lowest parts, that visible physical things should come down from invisible spiritual, and Adoil came down very great, and I beheld him, and lo! He had a belly of great light.

2 And I said to him: Become undone, Adoil, and let the visible physical come out of you.

3 And he came undone, and a great light came out. And I was in the midst of the great light, and as there is born light from light, there came forth a great age, and showed all creation, which I had thought to create.

---

[1] One book for each day of the year (leap year).

Seferim Khanok

4 And I saw that it was good.

5 And I placed for myself a throne, and took my seat on it, and said to the light: Go there up higher and fix yourself high above the throne, and be A foundation to the highest things.

6 And above the light there is nothing else, and then I bent up and looked up from my throne.

Chapter 26
1 And I summoned the very lowest a second time, and said: Let Archas come forth hard, and he came forth hard from the invisible spiritual.

2 And Archas came forth, hard, heavy, and very red.

3 And I said: Be opened, Archas, and let there be born from you, and he came undone, an age came forth, very great and very dark, bearing the creation of all lower things, and I saw that it was good and said to him:

4 Go there down below, and make yourself firm, and be a foundation for the lower things, and it happened and he went down and fixed himself, and became the foundation for the lower things, and below the darkness there is nothing else.

Chapter 27
1 And I commanded that there should be taken from light and darkness, and I said: Be thick, and it became thus, and I spread it out with the light, and it became water, and I spread it out over the darkness, below the light, and then I made firm the waters, that is to say the bottomless, and I made foundation of light around the water, and created seven circles from inside, and imaged the water like crystal wet and dry, that is to say like glass, and the circumcession of the waters and the other elements, and I showed each one of them its road, and the seven stars each one of them in its shamayim, that they go thus, and I saw that it was good.

Seferim Khanok

2 And I separated between light and between darkness, that is to say in the midst of the water hither and thither, and I said to the light, that it should be the day, and to the darkness, that it should be the night, and there was evening and there was morning the first day.

Chapter 28
1 And then I made firm the heavenly circle, and made that the lower water which is under shamayim collect itself together, into one whole, and that the chaos become dry, and it became so.

2 Out of the waves I created rock hard and big, and from the rock I piled up the dry, and the dry I called eretz, and the midst of the eretz I called abyss, that is to say the bottomless, I collected the sea in one place and bound it together with a yoke.

3 And I said to the sea: Behold I give you your eternal limits, and you shall not break loose from your component parts.

4 Thus I made fast the firmament. This day I called the first-created day.

Chapter 29
1 And for all the heavenly troops I imaged the image and essence of fire, and my eye looked at the very hard, firm rock, and from the gleam of my eye the lightning received its wonderful nature, which is both fire in water and water in fire, and one does not put out the other, nor does the one dry up the other, therefore the lightning is brighter than the sun, softer than water and firmer than hard rock.

2 And from the rock I cut off a great fire, and from the fire I created the orders of the incorporeal ten troops of malakhim, and their weapons are fiery and their raiment a burning flame, and I commanded that each one should stand in his order.

3 And one from out the order of malakhim, having turned away with the order that was under him, conceived an impossible thought, to place his throne higher than the

Seferim Khanok

clouds above the eretz, that he might become equal in rank to my power.

4 And I threw him out from the height with his malakhim, and he was flying in the air continuously above the bottomless.

Chapter 30

1 On the third day I commanded the eretz to make grow great and fruitful trees, and hills, and seed to sow, and I planted Paradise, and enclosed it, and placed as armed guardians flaming malakhim, and thus I created renewal.

2 Then came evening, and came morning the fourth day.

3 On the fourth day I commanded that there should be great lights on the heavenly circles.

4 On the first uppermost circle I placed the stars, Kruno, and on the second Aphrodit, on the third Aris, on the fifth Zoues, on the sixth Ermis, on the seventh lesser the moon, and adorned it with the lesser stars.

5 And on the lower I placed the sun for the illumination of day, and the moon and stars for the illumination of night.

6 The sun that it should go according to each constellation, twelve, and I appointed the succession of the months and their names and lives, their thunderings, and their hour-markings, how they should succeed.

7 Then evening came and morning came the fifth day.

8 On the fifth day I commanded the sea, that it should bring forth fishes, and feathered birds of many varieties, and all animals creeping over the eretz, going forth over the eretz on four legs, and soaring in the air, male sex and female, and every soul breathing the ruakh of life.

9 And there came evening, and there came morning the sixth day.

10 On the sixth day I commanded my wisdom to create man from seven consistencies: one, his flesh from the eretz; two, his blood from the dew; three, his eyes from the sun; four, his bones from stone; five, his intelligence from the swiftness of the malakhim and from cloud; six, his veins and his hair from the grass of the eretz; seven, his soul from my breath and from the wind.

11 And I gave him seven natures: to the flesh hearing, the eyes for sight, to the soul smell, the veins for touch, the blood for taste, the bones for endurance, to the intelligence sweetness.

12 I conceived a cunning saying to say, I created man from invisible spiritual and from visible physical nature, of both are his death and life and image, he knows speech like some created thing, small in greatness and again great in smallness, and I placed him on eretz, a second malakh, honourable, great and esteemed, and I appointed him as ruler to rule on eretz and to have my wisdom, and there was none like him of eretz of all my existing creatures.

13 And I appointed him a name, from the four component parts, from east, from west, from south, from north, and I appointed for him four special stars, and I called his name Ahdahm, and showed him the two ways, the light and the darkness, and I told him:

14 This is good, and that bad, that I should learn whether he has love towards me, or hatred, that it be clear which in his race love me.

15 For I have seen his nature, but he has not seen his own nature, therefore through not seeing he will transgression worse, and I said After transgression what is there but death?

16 And I put sleep into him and he fell asleep. And I took from him A rib, and created him a wife, that death should come to him by his wife, and I took his last word and called her name mother, that is to say, Khawa.

Chapter 31
1 Adam has life on eretz, and I created a garden in Ayden in the east, that he should observe the covenant and keep the command.

Seferim Khanok

2 I made the shamayim open to him, that he should see the malakhim singing the song of victory, and the gloomless light.

3 And he was continuously in paradise, and the devil understood that I wanted to create another world, because Ahdahm was Master on eretz, to rule and control it.

4 The devil is the evil ruakh of the lower places, as a fugitive he made Sotona from the shamayim as his name was Satanail HaStan, thus he became different from the malakhim, but his nature did not change his intelligence as far as his understanding of right-ruling and sinful things.

5 And he understood his condemnation and the transgression which he had sinned before, therefore he conceived thought against Ahdahm, in such form he entered and seduced Khawa, but did not touch Ahdahm.

6 But I cursed ignorance, but what I had magnified previously, those I did not curse, I cursed not man, nor the eretz, nor other creatures, but man's evil fruit, and his works.

Chapter 32
1 I said to him: Eretz you are, and into the eretz whence I took you, you shall go, and I will not ruin you, but send you from where I took you.

2 Then I can again receive you at My second presence.

3 And I put increases on all my creatures visible physical and invisible spiritual. And Ahdahm was five and half hours in paradise.

4 And I magnified the seventh day, which is the Sabbath, on which he rested from all his works.

Chapter 33
1 And I appointed the eighth day also, that the eighth day should be the first-created after my work, and that the first seven revolve in the form of the seventh thousand, and that at the beginning of the eighth thousand there should

be a time of not-counting, endless, with neither years nor months nor weeks nor days nor hours.

2 And now, Khanok, all that I have told you, all that you have understood, all that you have seen of heavenly things, all that you have seen on eretz, and all that I have written in books by my great wisdom, all these things I have devised and created from the uppermost foundation to the lower and to the end, and there is no counsellor nor inheritor to my creations.
3 I am self-eternal, not made with hands, and without change.

4 My thought is my counsellor, my wisdom and my word are made, and my eyes observe all things how they stand here and tremble with terror.

5 If I turn away my face, then all things will be destroyed.

6 And apply your mind, Khanok, and know him who is speaking to you, and take there the books which you yourself have written.

7 And I give you Samuil and Raguil, who led you up, and the books, and go down to eretz, and tell your sons all that I have told you, and all that you have seen, from the lower shamayim up to my throne, and all the troops.

8 For I created all forces, and there is none that resists me or that does not subject himself to me. For all subject themselves to my monarchy, and labour for my sole rules.

9 Give them the books of the handwriting, and they will read them and will know me for the creator of all things, and will understand how there is no other Elohim but me.

10 And let them distribute the books of your handwriting– children to children, generation to generation, nations to nations.

11 And I will give you, Khanok, my intercessor, the chief malakh Micha'el, for the handwritings of your fathers Ahdahm, Sheth, Enosh, Qaynan, Mahaleleel, and Yered your father.

Chapter 34

1 They have rejected my commandments and my yoke, worthless seed has come up, not fearing Elohim, and they would not bow down to me, but have begun to bow down to vain mighty ones, and denied my unity, and have laden the whole eretz with untruths, offences, abominable lecheries, namely one with another, and all manner of other unclean wickedness, which are disgusting to relate.

2 And therefore I will bring down a deluge upon the eretz and will destroy all men, and the whole eretz will crumble together into great darkness.

Seferim Khanok

Chapter 35
1 Behold from their seed shall arise another generation, much afterwards, but of them many will be very insatiate.
2 He who raises that generation, shall reveal to them the books of your handwriting, of your fathers, to them to whom he must point out the guardianship of the world, to the faithful men and workers of my pleasure, who do not acknowledge my name in vain.

3 And they shall tell another generation, and those others having read shall be esteemed thereafter, more than the first.

Chapter 36
1 Now, Khanok, I give you the term of thirty days to spend in your house, and tell your sons and all your household, that all may hear from my face what is told them by you, that they may read and understand, how there is no other Elohim but me.

2 And that they may always keep my commandments, and begin to read and take in the books of your handwriting.

3 And after thirty days I shall send my malakh for you, and he will take you from eretz and from your sons to me.

Chapter 37
1 And the Master called upon one of the older malakhim, terrible and menacing, and placed him by me, in appearance white as snow, and his hands like ice, having the appearance of great frost, and he froze my face, because I could not endure the terror of the Master, just as it is not possible to endure A stove's fire and the sun's heat, and the frost of the air.

2 And the Master said to me: Khanok, if your face be not frozen here, no man will be able to behold your face.

Chapter 38
1 And the Master said to those men who first led me up: Let Khanok go down on to eretz with you, and await him till the determined day.

2 And they placed me by night on my bed.

3 And Mathusal Metushelakh expecting my coming, keeping watch by day and by night at my bed, was filled with awe when he heard my coming, and I told him, Let all my household come together, that I tell them everything.

Chapter 39

1 Oh my children, my beloved ones, hear the admonition of your father, as much as is according to the Master's will.

2 I have been let come to you to-day, and announce to you, not from my lips, but from the Master's lips, all that is and was and all that is now, and all that will be till judgment-day.

3 For the Master has let me come to you, you hear therefore the words of my lips, of a man made big for you, but I am one who has seen the Master's face, like iron made to glow from fire it sends forth sparks and burns.

4 You look now upon my eyes, the eyes of a man big with meaning for you, but I have seen the Master's eyes, shining like the sun's rays and filling the eyes of man with awe.

5 You see now, my children, the right hand of a man that helps you, but I have seen the Master's right hand filling shamayim as he helped me.

6 You see the compass of my work like your own, but I have seen the Master's limitless and perfect compass, which has no end.

7 You hear the words of my lips, as I heard the words of the Master, like great thunder incessantly with hurling of clouds.

8 And now, my children, hear the discourses of the father of the eretz, how fearful and awful it is to come before the face of the ruler of the eretz, how much more terrible and awful it is to come before the face of the ruler of shamayim, the controller judge of quick and dead, and of the heavenly troops. Who can endure that endless pain?

Chapter 40

Seferim Khanok

1 And now, my children, I know all things, for this is from the Master's lips, and this my eyes have seen, from beginning to end.

2 I know all things, and have written all things into books, the heavens and their end, and their plenitude, and all the armies and their marchings.

3 I have measured and described the stars, the great countless multitude of them.

4 What man has seen their revolutions, and their entrances? For not even the malakhim see their number, while I have written all their names.

5 And I measured the sun's circle, and measured its rays, counted the
hours, I wrote down too all things that go over the eretz, I have written the things that are nourished, and all seed sown and unsown, which the eretz produces and all plants, and every grass and every flower, and their sweet smells, and their names, and the dwelling-places of the clouds, and their composition, and their wings, and how they bear rain and raindrops.

6 And I investigated all things, and wrote the road of the thunder and of the lightning, and they showed me the keys and their guardians, their rise, the way they go; it is let out gently in measure by a chain, lest by A heavy chain and violence it hurl down the angry clouds and destroy all things on eretz.

7 I wrote the treasure-houses of the snow, and the store-houses of the cold and the frosty airs, and I observed their season's key-holder, he fills the clouds with them, and does not exhaust the treasure-houses.

8 And I wrote the resting-places of the winds and observed and saw how their key-holders bear weighing-scales and measures; first, they put them in one weighing-scale, then in the other the weights and let them out according to measure cunningly over the whole eretz, lest by heavy breathing they make the eretz to rock.

Seferim Khanok

9 And I measured out the whole eretz, its mountains, and all hills, fields, trees, stones, rivers, all existing things I wrote down, the height from eretz to the seventh shamayim, and downwards to the very lowest hell, and the judgment-place, and the very great, open and weeping hell.

10 And I saw how the prisoners are in pain, expecting the limitless judgment.

11 And I wrote down all those being judged by the judge, and all their judgment and sentences and all their works.

Chapter 41
1 And I saw all forefathers from all time with Ahdahm and Khawa, and I sighed and broke into tears and said of the ruin of their dishonour:

2 Woe is me for my infirmity and for that of my forefathers, and thought in my heart and said:

3 Benevolent is the man who has not been born or who has been born and shall not transgression before the Master's face, that he come not into this place, nor bring the yoke of this place.

Chapter 42
1 I saw the key-holders and guards of the gates of sheol standing, like great serpents, and their faces like extinguishing lamps, and their eyes of fire, their sharp teeth, and I saw all the Master's works, how they are right, while the works of man are some good, and others bad, and in their works are known those who lie evilly.

Chapter 43
1 I, my children, measured and wrote out every work and every measure and every right-ruling judgment.

2 As one year is more honourable than another, so is one man more honourable than another, some for great possessions, some for wisdom of heart, some for particular intellect, some for cunning, one for silence of lip, another for cleanliness, one for strength, another for comeliness, one for youth, another for sharp wit, one for shape of body, another for sensibility, let it be heard everywhere, but there is none better than he who fears Elohim, he shall be more esteemed in time to come.

Chapter 44
1 The Master with his hands having created man, in the likeness of his own face, the Master made him small and great.

2 Whoever reviles the ruler's face, and abhors the Master's face, has despised the Master's face, and he who vents anger on any man without injury, the Master's great anger will cut him down, he who spits on the face of man reproachfully, will be cut down at the Master's great judgment.

3 Benevolent is the man who does not direct his heart with malice against any man, and helps the injured and condemned, and raises the broken down, and shall do charity to the needy, because on the day of the great judgment every weight, every measure and every makeweight will be as in the market, that is to say they are hung on scales and stand in the market, and every one shall learn his own measure, and according to his measure shall take his reward.

Chapter 45
1 Whoever hastens to make offerings before the Master's face, the Master for his part will hasten that offering by granting of his work.

2 But whoever increases his lamp before the Master's face and make not true judgment, the Master will not increase his treasure in the realm of the highest.

3 When the Master demands bread, or candles, or the flesh of beasts, or any other sacrifice, then that is nothing; but Elohim demands pure hearts, and with all that only tests the heart of man.

Chapter 46
1 Hear, my people, and take in the words of my lips.

Seferim Khanok

2 If any one bring any gifts to an earthly ruler, and have disloyal thoughts in his heart, and the ruler know this, will he not be angry with him, and not refuse his gifts, and not give him over to judgment?

3 Or if one man make himself appear good to another by deceit of tongue, but have evil in his heart, then will not the other understand the treachery of his heart, and himself be condemned, since his untruth was plain to all?

4 And when the Master shall send a great light, then there will be judgment for the just and the unjust, and there no one shall escape notice.

Chapter 47

1 And now, my children, lay thought on your hearts, mark well the words of your father, which are all come to you from the Master's lips.

2 Take these books of your father's handwriting and read them.

3 For the books are many, and in them you will learn all the Master's works, all that has been from the beginning of creation, and will be till the end of time.

4 And if you will observe my handwriting, you will not transgression against the Master; because there is no other except the Master, neither in shamayim, nor in eretz, nor in the very lowest places, nor in the one foundation.

5 The Master has placed the foundations in the unknown, and has spread forth heavens visible physical and invisible spiritual; he fixed the eretz on the waters, and created countless creatures, and who has counted the water and the foundation of the unfixed, or the dust of the eretz, or the sand of the sea, or the drops of the rain, or the morning dew, or the wind's breathings? Who has filled eretz and sea, and the indissoluble winter?

6 I cut the stars out of fire, and decorated shamayim, and put it in their midst.

Chapter 48

1 That the sun go along the seven heavenly circles, which are the appointment of one hundred and eighty-two

Seferim Khanok

thrones, that it go down on a short day, and again one hundred and eighty-two, that it go down on a big day, and he has two thrones on which he rests, revolving hither and thither above the thrones of the months, from the seventeenth day of the month Sivan it goes down to the month Thevan, from the seventeenth of Thevan it goes up.

2 And thus it goes close to the eretz, then the eretz is glad and makes grow its fruits, and when it goes away, then the eretz is sad, and trees and all fruits have no florescence.

3 All this he measured, with good measurement of hours, and fixed A measure by his wisdom, of the visible physical and the invisible spiritual.

4 From the invisible spiritual he made all things visible physical, himself being invisible spiritual.

5 Thus I make known to you, my children, and distribute the books to your children, into all your generations, and amongst the nations who shall have the sense to fear Elohim, let them receive them, and may they come to love them more than any food or earthly sweets, and read them and apply themselves to them.
6 And those who understand not the Master, who fear not Elohim, who accept not, but reject, who do not receive the books, a terrible judgment awaits these.

7 Benevolent is the man who shall bear their yoke and shall drag them along, for he shall be released on the day of the great judgment.

Chapter 49
1 I swear to you, my children, but I swear not by any oath, neither by shamayim nor by eretz, nor by any other creature which Elohim created.

2 The Master said: There is no oath in me, nor injustice, but truth.

3 If there is no truth in men, let them swear by the words, Yea, yea, or else, Nay, nay.

Seferim Khanok

4 And I swear to you, yes, yes, that there has been no man in his mother's womb, but that already before, even to each one there is a place prepared for the repose of that soul, and a measure fixed how much it is intended that a man be tried in this world.

5 Yes, children, deceive not yourselves, for there has been previously prepared a place for every soul of man.

Chapter 50

1 I have put every man's work in writing and none born on eretz can remain hidden nor his works remain concealed.

2 I see all things.

3 Now therefore, my children, in patience and meekness spend the number of your days, that you inherit endless life.

4 Endure for the sake of the Master every wound, every injury, every evil word and attack.

5 If ill-requitals befall you, return them not either to neighbour or enemy, because the Master will return them for you and be your avenger on the day of great judgment, that there be no avenging here among men.

6 Whoever of you spends gold or silver for his brother's sake, he will receive ample treasure in the world to come.

7 Injure not widows nor orphans nor strangers, lest Elohim's wrath come upon you.

Chapter 51

1 Stretch out your hands to the poor according to your strength.

2 Hide not your silver in the eretz.

3 Help the faithful man in affliction, and affliction will not find you in the time of your trouble.

4 And every grievous and cruel yoke that come upon you bear all for the sake of the Master, and thus you will find your reward in the day of judgment.

5 It is good to go morning, midday, and evening into the Master's dwelling, for the esteem of your creator.

6 Because every breathing thing glorifies him, and every creature visible physical and invisible spiritual returns him praise.

Chapter 52

1 Increased is the man who opens his lips in praise of Elohim of Sabaoth and praises the Master with his heart.

2 Cursed every man who opens his lips for the bringing into contempt and calumny of his neighbour, because he brings Elohim into contempt.

3 Increased is he who opens his lips magnifying and praising Elohim.

4 Cursed is he before the Master all the days of his life, who opens his lips to curse and abuse.

5 Increased is he who blesses all the Master's works.

6 Cursed is he who brings the Master's creation into contempt.

7 Increased is he who looks down and raises the fallen.

8 Cursed is he who looks to and is eager for the destruction of what is not his.

9 Increased is he who keeps the foundations of his fathers made firm from the beginning.

10 Cursed is he who perverts the decrees of his forefathers.
11 Increased is he who imparts shalom and love.

12 Cursed is he who disturbs those that love their neighbours.

13 Increased is he who speaks with humble tongue and heart to all.

14 Cursed is he who speaks shalom with his tongue, while in his heart there is no shalom but a sword.

15 For all these things will be laid bare in the weighing-scales and in the books, on the day of the great judgment.

Seferim Khanok

Chapter 53

1 And now, my children, do not say: Our father is standing before Elohim, and is praying for our sins, for there is there no helper of any man who has sinned.

2 You see how I wrote all works of every man, before his creation, all that is done amongst all men for all time, and none can tell or relate my handwriting, because the Master see all imaginings of man, how they are vain, where they lie in the treasure-houses of the heart.

3 And now, my children, mark well all the words of your father, that I tell you, lest you regret, saying: Why did our father not tell us?

Chapter 54

1 At that time, not understanding this let these books which I have given you be for an inheritance of your shalom.

2 Hand them to all who want them, and instruct them, that they may see the Master's very great and marvellous works.

Chapter 55

1 My children, behold, the day of my term and time have approached.
2 For the malakhim who shall go with me are standing before me and urge me to my departure from you; they are standing here on eretz, awaiting what has been told them.

3 For to-morrow I shall go up on to shamayim, to the uppermost Jerusalem to my eternal inheritance.

4 Therefore I bid you do before the Master's face all his good pleasure.

Chapter 56

1 Metushelakh having answered his father Khanok, said: What is agreeable to your eyes, father, that I may make before your face, that you may consecrate our dwellings, and your sons, and that your people may be made esteemed through you, and then that you may depart thus, as the Master said?

Seferim Khanok

2 Khanok answered to his son Metushelakh and said: Hear, child, from the time when the Master anointed me with the ointment of his esteem, there has been no food in me, and my soul remembers not earthly enjoyment, neither do I want anything earthly.

Chapter 57
1 My child Metushelakh, summon all your brethren and all your household and the elders of the people, that I may talk to them and depart, as is planned for me.

2 And Metushelakh made haste, and summoned his brethren, Regim, Riman, Uchan, Chermion, Gaidad, and all the elders of the people before the face of his father Khanok; and he Increased them, and said to them:

Chapter 58
1 Listen to me, my children, today.

2 In those days when the Master came down on to eretz for Ahdahm's sake, and visited all his creatures, which he created himself, after all these he created Ahdahm, and the Master called all the beasts of the eretz, all the reptiles, and all the birds that soar in the air, and brought them all before the face of our father Ahdahm.

3 And Ahdahm gave the names to all things living on eretz.

4 And the Master appointed him ruler over all, and subjected to him all things under his hands, and made them dumb and made them dull that they be commanded of man, and be in subjection and obedience to him.

5 Thus also the Master created every man Master over all his possessions.

6 The Master will not judge a single soul of beast for man's sake, but adjudges the souls of men to their beasts in this world; for men have a special place.

7 And as every soul of man is according to number, similarly beasts will not perish, nor all souls of beasts which the Master created, till the great judgment, and they will accuse man, if he feed them ill.

Seferim Khanok

Chapter 59
1 Whoever defiles the soul of beasts, defiles his own soul.

2 For man brings clean animals to make sacrifice for transgression, that he may have cure of his soul.

3 And if they bring for sacrifice clean animals, and birds, man has cure, he cures his soul.

4 All is given you for food, bind it by the four feet, that is to make good the cure, he cures his soul.

5 But whoever kills beast without wounds kills his own souls and defiles his own flesh.

6 And he who does any beast any injury whatsoever, in secret, it is evil practice, and he defiles his own soul.

Chapter 60
1 He who works the killing of a man's soul, kills his own soul, and kills his own body, and there is no cure for him for all time.

2 He who puts a man in any snare shall stick in it himself, and there is no cure for him for all time.

3 He who puts a man in any vessel, his retribution will not be wanting at the great judgment for all time.

4 He who works crookedly or speaks evil against any soul will not make justice for himself for all time.

Chapter 61
1 And now, my children keep your hearts from every injustice, which the Master hates. Just as a man asks something for his own soul from Elohim, so let him do to every living soul, because I know all things, how in the great time to come there is much inheritance prepared for men, good for the good, and bad for the bad, without number many.

2 Increased are those who enter the good houses, for in the bad houses there is no shalom nor return from them.

Seferim Khanok

3 Hear, my children, small and great! When man puts a good thought in his heart, brings gifts from his labours before the Master's face and his hands made them not, then the Master will turn away his face from the labour of his hand, and that man cannot find the labour of his hands.

4 And if his hands made it, but his heart murmur, and his heart cease not making murmur incessantly, he has not any advantage.

Chapter 62
1 Increased is the man who in his patience brings his gifts with faith before the Master's face, because he will find forgiveness of sins.
2 But if he takes back his words before the time, there is no repentance for him; and if the time pass and he do not of his own will what is promised, there is no repentance after death.
3 Because every work which man does before the time, is all deceit before men, and transgression before Elohim.

Chapter 63
1 When man clothes the naked and fills the hungry, he will find reward from Elohim.

2 But if his heart murmurs, he commits a double evil; ruin of himself and of that which he gives; and for him there will be no finding of reward on account of that.

3 And if his own heart is filled with his food and his own flesh, clothed with his own clothing, he commits contempt, and will forfeit all his endurance of poverty, and will not find reward of his good deeds.
4 Every proud and magniloquent man is hateful to the Master, and every false speech, clothed in untruth; it will be cut with the blade of the sword of death, and thrown into the fire, and shall burn for all time.

Chapter 64
1 When Khanok had spoken these words to his sons, all people far and near heard how the Master was calling Khanok. They took counsel together:

Seferim Khanok

2 Let us go and kiss Khanok, and two thousand men came together and came to the place Achuzan where Khanok was, and his sons.

3 And the elders of the people, the whole assembly, came and bowed down and began to kiss Khanok and said to him:

4 Our father Khanok, may you be Increased of the Master, the eternal ruler, and now consecrate your sons and all the people, that we may be esteemed to-day before your face.

5 For you shall be esteemed before the Master's face for all time, since the Master chose you, rather than all men on eretz, and designated you writer of all his creation, visible physical and invisible spiritual, and redeemed of the sins of man, and helper of your household.

Chapter 65

1 And Khanok answered all his people saying: Hear, my children, before that all creatures were created, the Master created the visible physical and invisible spiritual things.

2 And as much time as there was and went past, understand that after all that he created man in the likeness of his own form, and put into him eyes to see, and ears to hear, and heart to reflect, and intellect wherewith to deliberate.

3 And the Master saw all man's works, and created all his creatures, and divided time, from time he fixed the years, and from the years he appointed the months, and from the months he appointed the days, and of days he appointed seven.

4 And in those he appointed the hours, measured them out exactly, that man might reflect on time and count years, months, and hours, their alternation, beginning, and end, and that he might count his own life, from the beginning until death, and reflect on his transgression and write his work bad and good; because no work is hidden before the Master, that every man might know his works and never transgress all his commandments, and keep my handwriting from generation to generation.

Seferim Khanok

5 When all creation visible physical and invisible spiritual, as the Master created it, shall end, then every man goes to the great judgment, and then all time shall perish, and the years, and thenceforward there will be neither months nor days nor hours, they will be adhered together and will not be counted.

6 There will be one age, and all the right-ruling who shall escape the Master's great judgment, shall be collected in the great age, for the right-ruling the great age will begin, and they will live eternally, and then too there will be amongst them neither labour, nor sickness, nor humiliation, nor anxiety, nor need, nor brutality, nor night, nor darkness, but great light.

7 And they shall have a great indestructible wall, and a paradise bright and incorruptible eternal, for all corruptible mortal things shall pass away, and there will be eternal life.

Chapter 66
1 And now, my children keep your souls from all injustice, such as the Master hates.

2 Walk before his face with terror and trembling and serve him alone.

3 Bow down to the true Elohim, not to dumb idols, but bow down to his similitude, and bring all just offerings before the Master's face. The Master hates what is unjust. [1]

4 For the Master sees all things; when man takes thought in his heart, then he counsels the intellects, and every thought is always before the Master, who made firm the eretz and put all creatures on it.

5 If you look to shamayim, the Master is there; if you take thought of the sea's deep and all the under-eretz, the Master is there.

---

[1] Many are still being unjust to each other need to repent and return back to the Torah of YHWH.

Seferim Khanok

6 For the Master created all things. Bow not down to things made by man, leaving the Master of all creation, because no work can remain hidden before the Master's face.

7 Walk, my children, in long-suffering, in meekness, honesty,[1] in provocation, in grief, in faith and in truth, in reliance on promises, in illness, in abuse, in wounds, in temptation, in nakedness, in privation, loving one another, till you go out from this age of ills, that you become inheritors of endless time.

8 Increased are the just who shall escape the great judgment, for they shall shine forth more than the sun sevenfold, for in this world the seventh part is taken off from all, light, darkness, food, enjoyment, sorrow, paradise, torture, fire, frost, and other things; he put all down in writing, that you might read and understand.

Chapter 67

1 When Khanok had talked to the people, the Master sent out darkness on to the eretz, and there was darkness, and it covered those men standing with Khanok, and they took Khanok up on to the highest shamayim, where the Master is; and he received him and placed him before his face, and the darkness went off from the eretz, and light came again.

2 And the people saw and understood not how Khanok had been taken, and esteemed Elohim, and found a roll in which was traced The Invisible spiritual Elohim; and all went to their dwelling places.

Chapter 68

1 Khanok was born on the sixth day of the month Sivan, and lived three hundred and sixty-five years.

2 He was taken up to shamayim on the first day of the month Sivan and remained in shamayim sixty days.

3 He wrote all these signs of all creation, which the Master created, and wrote three hundred and sixty-six books, and

---

[1] Honesty is lacking in many and a virtue that needs to be strongly adhered to grow the kingdom of Elohim.

handed them over to his sons and remained on eretz thirty days, and was again taken up to shamayim on the sixth day of the month Sivan, on the very day and hour when he was born.

4 As every man's nature in this life is dark, so are also his conception, birth, and departure from this life.

5 At what hour he was conceived, at that hour he was born, and at that hour too he died.

6 Metushelakh and his brethren, all the sons of Khanok, made haste, and erected an altar at that place called Achuzan, whence and where Khanok had been taken up to shamayim.

7 And they took sacrificial oxen and summoned all people and sacrificed the sacrifice before the Master's face.

8 All people, the elders of the people and the whole assembly came to the feast and brought gifts to the sons of Khanok.

9 And they made a great feast, rejoicing and making merry three days, praising Elohim, who had given them such a sign through Khanok, who had found favour with him, and that they should hand it on to their sons from generation to generation, from age to age.

10 Amein

Seferim Khanok

The scroll of Three Khanok 3 Khanok

**By Rabbi Y'shma'el Ben Elisha
The High Priest**

Chapter 1

INTRODUCTION:
R. Y'shma'el ascends

To shamayim to behold the vision of the Merkaba and is given in charge to Metatron

Beresheeth 5:24 And Khanok Walked With Elohim: And He Was Not; For Elohim Took Him

Rabbi Y'shma'el said:

1 When I ascended on high to behold the vision of the Merkaba and had entered the six Halls, one within the other:

2 As soon as I reached the door of the seventh Hall I stood still in petition before the Set-apart One, Increased be he, and, lifting up my eyes on high i.e. towards the Divine Majesty, I said:

3 "Master of the Universe, I petition thee, that the merit of Aharon, the son of Amram, the lover of shalom and pursuer of shalom, who received the crown of priesthood from Your Esteem on the mount of Sinai, be valid for me in this hour, so that Qafsiel, the prince, and the malakhim with him may not get power over me nor throw me down from the shamayim.

4 Forthwith the Set-apart One, magnified be He, sent to me Metatron, his Servant 'Ebed the malakh, the Prince of the Presence, and be, spreading his wings, with great joy came to meet me so as to save me from their hand.

Seferim Khanok

5 And he took me by his band in their sight, saying to me: "Enter in shalom before the high and exalted King and behold the picture of the Merkaba."

6 Then I entered the seventh Hall, and he led me to the camps of Shekina and placed me before the Set-apart One, magnified be He, to behold the Merkaba.

7 As soon as the princes of the Merkaba and the flaming Seraphim perceived me, they fixed their eyes upon me. Instantly trembling and shuddering seized me and I fell down and was benumbed by the radiant image of their eyes and the splendid appearance of their faces; until the Set-apart One, magnified be He, rebuked them, saying:

8 "My servants, my Seraphim, my Cherubim and my 'Ophannim! Cover ye your eyes before Y'shma'el, my son, my friend, my beloved one and my esteem, that he tremble not nor shudder!"

9 Forthwith Metatron the Prince of the Presence, came and restored my ruakh and put me upon my feet.

10 After that moment there was not in me strength enough to say a song before the Throne of Esteem of the esteemed King, the mightiest of all kings, the most excellent of all princes, until after the hour had passed.

11 After one hour had passed the Set-apart One, magnified be He, opened to me the gates of Shekina, the gates of Shalom, the gates of Wisdom, the gates of Strength, the gates of Power, the gates of Speech Dibbur, the gates of Song, the gates of Qedusha, the gates of Chant.

12 And he enlightened my eyes and my heart by words of psalm, song, praise, exaltation, thanksgiving, extolment, glorification, hymn and eulogy. And as I opened my mouth, uttering a song before the Set-apart One, magnified be He, the Set-apart Chayyoth (lives) beneath and above the Throne of Esteem answered and said: "Kadosh" and "Benevolent is The esteem of YHVH From His Place!" i.e. chanted the Qedusha.

Seferim Khanok

Chapter 2
The highest classes of malakhim make inquiries about R. Y'shma'el, which are answered by Metatron

R.Y'shma'el said:
1 In that hour the eagles of the Merkaba, the flaming 'Ophannim and the Seraphim of consuming fire asked Metatron, saying to him:

2 Youth, why do you permit one born of woman to enter and behold the Merkaba? From which nation, from which tribe is this one? What is his character?" Metatron answered and said to them: "From the nation of Israel whom the Set-apart One, Benevolent be He, chose for his people

3 From among seventy tongues nations, from the tribe of Lewi, whom he set aside as a contribution to his name and from the seed of Aharon whom the Set-apart One, Benevolent be He, did choose for his servant and put upon him the crown of priesthood on. "

4 Forthwith they spoke and said: "Indeed, this one is worthy to behold the Merkaba". And they said: "Happy are the people that is in such a case!" Tehilim (Psalm) 144:15.

Chapter 3
Metatron has 70 names, but Elohim calls him 'Youth'
R.Y'shma'el said:

1 In that hour I asked Metatron, the malakh, the Prince of the Presence: "What is your name?" **2** He answered me: "I have seventy names, corresponding to the seventy tongues of the world and all of them are based upon the name Metatron, malakh of the Presence; but my King calls me 'Youth' Na'ar ".

Chapter 4
Metatron is identical with Khanok who was translated to shamayim at the time of the Deluge

R.Y'shma'el said:
1 I asked Metatron and said to him: "Why art you called by the name of your Creator, by severity names? You art

Seferim Khanok

greater than all the princes, higher than all the malakhim, beloved more than all the servants, honored above all the mighty ones in kingship, greatness and esteem: why do they call thee ' Youth 'in the high heavens? "

2 He answered and said to me: "Because I am Khanok, the son of Yered.

3 For when the generation of the flood sinned and were confounded in their deeds saying unto Elohim: ' Depart from us, for We desire not the knowledge of your ways Job 21:14', then the Set-apart One, Benevolent be He removed me from their midst to be a witness against them in the high heavens to all the inhabitants of the world that they may not say: ' The Merciful One is cruel'.

4 What sinned all those multitudes , their wives, their sons and their daughters, their horses, their mules and their cattle and their property, and all the birds of the world, all of which the Set-apart One, Benevolent be He, destroyed from their world together with them in the waters of the flood?
Nor may say: What though the generation of the flood did transgression; the beasts and the birds, what had they sinned, that they should perish with them?'

5 Hence the Set-apart One, Benevolent be He, lifted me up in their lifetime before their eyes to be a witness against them to the future world. And the Set-apart One, Benevolent be He, assigned me for a prince and a ruler among the ministering malakhim.

6 In that hour three of the ministering malakhim, 'UZZA, 'AZZA and 'AZZAEL[1] came forth and brought charges against me in the high heavens, saying before the Set-apart One, Benevolent be He " Said not the Ancient Ones First Ones rightly before Thee: 'Do not create man! '" The Set-apart One, Benevolent be He, answered and said unto them: "I have made and I will bear, yes, I will carry and will deliver". Yeshayahu (Isaiah) 46:4.

7 As soon as they saw me, they said before Him: "Master of the Universe! What is this one that he should ascend to

---

[1] Name of the rebellious angels.

Seferim Khanok

the height of heights? Is not he one from among the sons of [the sons of] those who perished in the days of the Flood? "What does he do in the Raqia (Heavens)'? "

8 Again, the Set-apart One, Benevolent be He, answered and said to them: "What are ye that ye enter and speak in my presence? I delight in this one more than in all of you, and hence he shall be a prince and a ruler over you in the high heavens."

9 Forthwith all stood up and went out to meet me, prostrated themselves before me and said: "Happy are you and happy is your father for your Creator does favor you".

10 And because I am small and a youth among them

11 In days, months and years, therefore they call me "Youth" Na'ar.

Chapter 5
The idolatry of the generation of Khanok causes Elohim to remove the Shekina from eretz The idolatry' inspired by 'Azza, 'Uzza and 'Azziel

R. Y'shma'el said: Metatron, the Prince of the Presence, said to me:

1 From the day when the Set-apart One, Benevolent be He, expelled the first Ahdahm from the Garden of Ayden and onwards, Shekina was dwelling upon a cherub under the Tree of Life. And the ministering malakhim

2 were gathering together and going down from shamayim in parties, from the Raqia' in companies and from the heavens in camps to do His will in the whole world.

3 And the first man and his generation were sitting outside the gate of the Garden to behold the radiant appearance of the Shekina.

4 For the splendor of the Shekina traversed the world from one end to the other with a splendor 365,000 times that of the globe of the sun. And everyone who made use of the splendor of the Shekina, on him no flies and no gnats did

Seferim Khanok

rest, neither was he ill nor suffered lie any pain. No demons got power over him, neither were they able to injure him.

5 When the Set-apart One, Benevolent be He, went out and went in from the Garden to Ayden, from Ayden to the Garden, from the Garden to Raqia' and from Raqia' to the Garden of Ayden then all and everyone beheld the splendor of His Shekina and they were not injured;

6 Until the time of the generation of Khanok who was the head of all idol worshippers of the world.

7 And what did the generation of Khanok do? They went from one end of the world to the other, and each one brought silver, gold, precious stones and pearls in heaps like unto mountains and hills making idols out of them throughout all the world. And they erected the idols in every quarter of the world: the size of each idol was 1000 parasangs.

8 And they brought down the sun, the moon, planets and constellations, and placed them before the idols on their right hand and on their left, to attend them even as they attend the Set-apart One, Benevolent be He, as it is written in First Kings 22:39: "And all the host of shamayim was standing by him on his right hand and on his left".
Verse 9 not numbered

10 In that time the ministering malakhim brought charges against them before the Set-apart One, Benevolent be He, saying before him:
"Master of the World! What have you to do with the children of men? As it is written Ps. 8:4 'What is man Khanok that you are mindful of him?' 'Mah Ahdahm' is not written here, but 'Mah Khanok', for he Khanok is the head of the idol worshippers.

11 Why have you left the highest of the high heavens, the abode of your esteemed Name, and the high and exalted Throne in 'Araboth on high and are gone and dwell with the children of men who worship idols and make you equal to the idols.

Seferim Khanok

12 Now you are on eretz and the idols likewise. What have you to do with the inhabitants of the eretz who worship idols?"

13 Forthwith the Set-apart One, Benevolent be He, lifted up His Shekina from the eretz, from their midst.

14 In that moment came the ministering malakhim, the troops of hosts and the armies of 'Araboth in thousand camps and ten thousand hosts: they fetched trumpets and took the horns in their hands and surrounded the Shekina with all kinds of songs. And He ascended to the high heavens, as it is written Ps. xlvii. 5: "Elohim is gone up with a shout, the Master with the sound of a trumpet".

Seferim Khanok

Chapter 6
Khanok lifted up to shamayim together with the Shekina.
Malakhim' protests answered by Elohim

R. Y'shma'el said: Metatron, the Malakh, the Prince of the Presence, said to me:

1 When the Set-apart One, Benevolent be He, desired to lift me up on high, He first sent 'Anaphiel Tetragrammaton, the Prince, and he took me from their midst in their sight and carried me in great esteem upon a fiery chariot with fiery horses, servants of esteem. And he lifted me up to the high heavens together with the Shekina.

2 As soon as I reached the high heavens, the Set-apart Chayyoth, the 'Ophannim, the Seraphim, the Cherubim, the Wheels of the Merkaba the Galgallim, and the ministers of 5th consuming fire, perceiving my smell from a distance of 365,000 myriads of parasangs, said:
"What smell of one born of woman and what taste of a white drop is this that ascends on high, and lo, he is merely a gnat among those who 'divide flames of fire'?"

3 The Set-apart One, Benevolent be he, answered and spake unto them: "My servants, my hosts, my Cherubim, my 'Ophaminim, my Seraphim! Be ye not displeased on account of this! Since all the children of men have denied me and my great Kingdom and are gone worshipping idols, I have removed my Shekina from among them and have lifted it up on high. But this one whom I have taken from among them is an ELECT ONE among the inhabitants of the world and he is equal to all of them in faith, right-ruling and perfection of deed and I have taken him for as a tribute from my world under all the heavens".

Chapter 7
Khanok raised upon the wings of the Shekina to the place of the Throne, the Merkaba and the angelic hosts

R. Y'shma'el said: Metatron, the Malakh, the Prince of the Presence, said to me:

When the Set-apart One, Benevolent be He, took me away from the generation of the Flood, he lifted me on the wings

Seferim Khanok

of the wind of Shekina to the highest shamayim and brought me into the great palaces of the 'Araboth Raqia' on high, where is the esteemed Throne of the Shekina, the Merkaba, the troops of anger, the armies of vehemence, the fiery Shin'anim, the flaming Cherubim, and the burning 'Ophannim,[1] the flaming servants, the flashing Chashmallim, and the lightening Seraphim. And he placed me there to attend the Throne of Esteem day after day.

The End of the scroll of fragments.

May the El of Y'sra'el guide you and increase those of you who obey His Torah.

Rabbi Simon Altaf Hakohen

-

---

[1] Types of malakhim.

Seferim Khanok

Glossary

YHWH	YHWH the sacred name of Elohim
Eretz	Eretz
Erev	Evening
Etz	Tree
Etzim	Trees
Kedushim/Qedushim	Saints
Mayim	Water
Ruakh	Spirit
Ruakhot	Ruakhot
Set-Apart	Set-apart
Siniyah	Mount Sinai in Saudi Arabia
Shalom	Peace with salvation, well being
Shamayim	Used both for the sky, space and place where YHWH dwells.
Tsadik	Right-ruling
Unclean Ruakhot	Demons

Seferim Khanok

Seferim Khanok

Seferim Khanok
We suggest you visit our website to see the following Titles:
www.african-israel.com

Beyth Yahushua – the Son of Tzadok, the Son of Dawud

Would you like to know the identity of Yahushua's family the man you call Jesus? Did He have brothers and sisters, did He get married, and are not Rabbis meant to marry?

Is it true if Mary Magdalene was His wife and if not then what relationship did she have with him?

Are you fed-up of hearing objections from unbelievers such as "since you do not know who Matthew, Mark, Luke and John were then how can you claim to have the truth?" Now you will know the truth without asking your pastor.

Who was Nicodemus and what relationship did Yahushua, Jesus of Nazareth have with Nicodemus? Who was the wider family of Yahushua?

For far too long He has been portrayed as the wandering man with no belongings and no family and living outside his home with women offering him money and food. This picture is both misleading and deceptive.

Do you want to know the powerful family of rebbe Yahushua that was a threat to Rome? They made him into a G-d/man.

Who were Mark, Luke, and Matthew? Was Luke a gentile or a Hebrew priest?

What about the genealogy of Luke and Matthew in which the two fathers of rebbe Yahushua mentioned are Heli or Jacob in Matthew chapter 1:16 and Luke chapter 3:23 respectively?

This book will give you new insights and the rich history of rebbe Yahushua.

Seferim Khanok

Islam, Peace or Beast

Have you ever wondered why radical Muslims are blowing up buildings, bombings planes and creating havoc? We illustrate in this book the reality of radical Islam and the end of days that are upon us. Why are our governments reluctant to tell us the truth we uncover many details.

World War III – Salvation of the Jews

- How will the salvation of the Jews come about, will they convert to Christianity or will Christianity be folded into Judaism?
- Will the 3rd Temple be built before the coming of the Messiah? Analyzed and explained with the correct sound hermeneutics.
- Will we have a war with Iran and when? Considering the pundits have been wrong since the last 3 years and only Simon has been on track up to this time. What signs will absolutely indicate impending war with Iran calculated and revealed.
- When will the Messiah come, what signs should we be looking for, is it on a Jubilee year?
- Will the Messiah come on the feast of Trumpets fact or fiction?
- Will America win the war in Afghanistan? Yes and No answer with details.
- Who is the prince of Ezekiel and why is he making sin sacrifices. Can one call these educational? Read the correct answers...
- Should we support the Jewish Aliyah to Israel or is it forbidden to enter the land for permanent stay under a secular G-dless government?

Rabbi Simon Altaf HaKohen is the only Rabbi to look at the thorny issues that no one has addressed to date while many people mostly run with popular churchy opinions coloured by bad theology by picking and choosing verses in isolation. Is modern Zionism biblical? Is Israel right to take over territories occupied by Palestinians today? Should people be selling up homes to go and live in

Seferim Khanok

Israel? All these thorny questions and even more answered in this book the sequel to the popular prophecy book World War III - Unmasking the End-Times Beast.

Dear Muslim – Meet YHWH the G-d of Abraham

Truth explained, best seller step by step detailing and unveiling Islam! This book is designed for that friend, son or daughter who is about to convert into Islam but needs to read this first. This is the one stop to saving their soul. Don't procrastinate, get it today so that they may see what is the truth before they cause themselves to be confounded and duped into something totally not true.

The Feasts of YHWH, the Elohim of Israel

Have you ever asked why the feasts were given to Israel as a people? What is the meaning of the festivals and what about their purpose which is all explained in this detailed book that delves into the signs of the feasts. Why are we to obey the feasts forever and if we do not then we could potentially lose our place in the kingdom entry! Well no one said that before but now you will see and experience an exhilarating experience of knowing what it is like to be there. How does it feel to be up all night to celebrate the festival of Shavuot (Pentecost), what does it mean and many other details.

Testament of Abraham

Now it's time to hear Abraham's story from his own mouth what happened, how did he become G-d's friend. What other missing information that we are not told about is made available. Without Abraham there will be no Judaism, no Islam and no Christianity. He is the pivotal point upon which all three religious text claim right but who does Abraham really belong to?

What is Truth?

Have you wondered what truth is and how we measure it? How do we arrive at the conclusion that what you have is truth? How do you know that the religion you have been following for so many years is the original faith? Can we

Seferim Khanok

examine Atheism and say why it is or is not true. We examine these things.

Hidden Truths Hebraic Scrolls Study Bible 5th Edition (Complete)

The HT Complete Bible more myths busted. Over 1300 pages packed absolutely full of information - no Hebrew roots Scriptures, even comes close this is guaranteed and these scrolls are the difference between night and day, see for yourself!!! The politically incorrect guide to the G-d of Israel and the real chosen people of YHWH. Are you willing to listen to what YHWH has said about our world and how He is going to restore all things back including His real chosen people hidden to this day?

Many texts uncovered and explained in great details accurately and many corrections made to the many faulty translations out there making this a real eye-opener text.

- ➔ Was Chava (Eve) the only woman in the garden? We reveal a deep held secret.
- ➔ Where did the demons come from?
- ➔ Ezekiel refers to some of Israel's evil deeds in Egypt explicitly uncovered which are glossed over in the King James Version.
- ➔ Who are the Real Hebrews of the Scriptures, which people does the land of Y'sra'el really belong to? Time to do away with the deception.
- ➔ Did Abraham keep the Sabbath? We show you when and where.
- ➔ But I thought Keturah was Hagar, another error of Judaism corrected.
- ➔ But I thought Keturah was married to Abraham after Sarah's death, no not really. A very bad textual translation in Genesis 25:1.
- ➔ Who was Balaam, a profit for cash as are many pastors and Bishops today doing the same thing running and chasing after the Almighty dollar?
- ➔ Who were Abraham's ancestors, Africans or Europeans?

Seferim Khanok

- → Why did Isaac marry at forty years of age, what happened to his first wife? Rebecca was not his only wife, an error and ignorance of Christendom exposed?
- → Where is Noah's ark likely to be? Not Ararat in Turkey or Iran another error.
- → Who are the four wives of Abraham and who is the real firstborn? Not Ishmael and not even Isaac. Was Isaac his only begotten son another error?
- → All the modification of modern Judaism of the scribes has been undone to give you what was the real text including the original conversation of the Serpent with Chava (Gen 3) unedited plus Abraham's conversation unedited at last in Genesis 18.

The legendary Rabbi Simon Altaf HaKohen, guarantees that this will teach you to take the best out there and open their eyes in prophecy, historical argument and theology. He will personally mentor you through the texts of the Torah, the prophets, the disciples and the apostles of Yahushua. Does any Scrolls-seller offer this extent of training? We do. And Rabbi Simon is available at the end of an e-mail, or just a telephone call away for questions that you have all this time; and if he is not there you just leave a message on the phone, and his promise is to get back to you anywhere in the world. We do not charge for our calls or any teachings over the phone. It does not matter if you are in India, Australia, Russia or the US or Timbuktu we will call you back.

Sefer Yashar (The Book of Jasher)
The book of Yashar has been translated from the original sources and with added commentary, corrected names of Elohim with the sacred names and with other missing text from the Hebrew. This will add to the gaps in your knowledge from the book of Genesis such as the following:
- What did the wicked do before the flood?
- Who were Abraham's African ancestors?
- Did Abraham have two wives?

Seferim Khanok
- What relationship did Abraham have with Eli'ezer?
- Did Isaac wait forty years to be married?
- Why did Sarah die so suddenly?
- Did Moses marry in Egypt?
- Moses, what colour? White or Black.
- Many other questions now answered.

Seferim Chanoch (The Books of Enoch)
The books of Enoch details the fall, the names of the angels, what happened in the beginning and what was the result of those fallen angels. Where are they now and what will happen to them. He also reveals the birth of Noach and some very important details around this about the African ancestry of the patriarchs. He reveals the Son of Elohim. And many other important details to complete your knowledge.

Yahushua – The Black Messiah
Have you been lied to about the true identity of rebbe Yahushua? Have you been shown pictures of the idolatrous Borgia Cesare and may have believed that this Caucasian hybrid was rebbe Yahushua? What ethnicity was Yahushua and what race of people did He belong to? Is it important that we know His ethnicity? What colour was Moses, King David and King Solomon? We examine and look at the massive fraud perpetrated upon the western nations by their leaders to hide the real identity of the true Hebrew Israelite people and race which are being restored in these Last Days.

Hebrew Wisdom – Kabbalah in the Brit ha Chadasha
The book's purpose is to illustrate basic principles of Kabbalah and to reveal some of the Kabbalah symbolisms used in the New Testament writings though they are not sacred. We look at the Sefirots what they mean and how they apply. We also look at the first chapter in Genesis and examine some of the symbols there. We examine the name of Elohim in Exodus 3:14 and see what it means.

Seferim Khanok

The Apocrypha (With Pirke Avot 'Ethics of The Fathers')

Read the fifteen books of the Apocrypha to get an understanding of the events both of the exile and of Israel's early history. Read Ethics of the Fathers to understand rabbinic wisdom and some important elements of the story of Genesis. The tests, the trials and the miracles of the Temples. Without these books, the story in the Scriptures are incomplete, and has gaps which these books will fill up and give you a more complete understanding.

African-Israel Siddur transliterated Hebrew with English (Daily life prayers)

Many times we wonder what prayers should we do when we go to bed, when we leave our home in the morning and how do we petition daily? What petitions should I do if I have a ritual bath? What petition is for affixing a Mezuzah? Each year you wonder how to do the Passover Aggadah and what is the procedure. This book also covers women's niddah laws to give you understanding into women's ritual purity. Unlike other petition books Rabbi Simon Altaf HaKohen, actually bothers to explain small details that are important and often ignored. This is one book you should not be without! Some important things such as for burial, graveyards, and many more details.

What Else Have They Kept From Us?

This book is as the result of an e-mail conversation with a believer who asked me some questions and one of her questions upon my answer was "What else have they kept from us?" This was the question that led to this book because instead of answering people with small sections of answers I decided the time had come that a book had to be written to answer and address everything as it occurred from the start to the end so that many may see that the deception is real and it's a deep cunning deception which starts from your TV screens, in your newspapers followed by wherever you go in your daily life. How would a person know that they are being deceived if they do not know what to look for? **Its like a Ten Pound note; well if you saw** the original then you have something to compare the false note with, but what if you were <u>never</u> presented with the original and always had the fake in your pocket, then you will likely think the fake is real and this is how it is with Christianity today, that is simply mixing paganism with truth. A false Ten pound note or a bad tender which will give you no value when you redeem it as I uncover it in the pages of this book.

Patriarchal Marriage, Y'sra'el's Right-Ruling Way of Life, Methods and Practice

How did the Y'sra'elites live? What form of marriage did they practice and how did they practice it? This book is about to show you what was G-d's design from the beginning and how the Y'sra'elites lived within G-d's required parameters. Today these things appear mythological but here we show you the methods and ways of how this lifestyle was practiced and is being restored in these last days while the much touted monogamy is wrecking lives and destroying families and society around us. How many marriages are breaking down as a result of the wrong model and how many children are living fatherless lives while women live husbandless and unfulfilled lives. This book will show you why the Greek and Roman monogamy model with a husband and a wife and a bit on the side does not work. While G-d's model of plural marriage is an everlasting model that not only works but saves many children from losing their father's and women from losing good husbands.

The Scroll of Yahubel (Jubilees)

The information that is missing in the Torah has been put in here to aid us in understanding the book of Genesis more. There are gaps in Genesis with what happened with Noakh? What was going on in Moses's time. This scroll allows us to piece together that information that is so important for our understanding. True names edition with many corrections made.

Seferim Khanok

Who am I?

A Children's book to help the black Hebrew children with identity and direction in life. Many Hebrew children while looking for identity easily stray. While they search for love they end up in gangs to prove themselves and search for that missing something. When they do not find love in their homes due to broken homes often venturing out with devastating consequences, getting involved in criminal activities to prove themselves ruining their lives. This book's purpose is to help these children and even adults find themselves to teach them who they are and to find sound direction in life to secure you to the G-d of our ancestors where you belong. This will help change many lives.

Hidden Truths Hebraic Scrolls Compendium Guide -

For those who have the Hidden-Truths Hebraic Scrolls this is a must buy to give you a deeper understanding under the text and its meaning where the footnotes are expounded upon further in various books of the scrolls.

Hebrew Characters, The Power to have prayers answered

Have you ever tried praying and find that either your prayers take very long time to answer or they don't get answered at all? In frustration you ask other friends to pray for you in hope that you may get an answer from G-d soon.

I have given considerable thought about the condition of our people and how many languish in poverty, in situations where they seek for help because they are given false dogmas, put in religious bondage and slavery of the mind and heart.

Many times they make their own lives harder because they have spent so much time in the nations that they just want to live like the gentiles and not Hebrew as they are unaware how to benefit themselves that await them. I know it can be a lonely road at times. Our Abbah in the heavens feels our pain while we live in exile He sends the Em Chomah to be with us. He longs for us to return back to the contracts that we may receive all the increases and benefits that are only meant for us.

However we pass our life by with this that and the other person who gives us no joy but we think maybe if we carry on suffering things will change for the better but things NEVER change. This

Seferim Khanok

book was written to help for a time such as this to better the lives of our people. To empower them with the right petitions to give them benefits and increases in employment, love, marriage and sickness. This will help you break the spells of witchcraft, dealing with jealous people around you and personal anger issues. This will help you deal with demonic presences in your homes. This will show you how to receive a timely answer to all your prayers. I have used these methods for my students all over the world which have proven successful for them and have greatly benefited them.

It takes many generations for a right-ruling priest to be born in our generations. How many generations our people have suffered the scourge of the curses for not obeying the Torah? Many are still suffering. The Most High is going to raise his priests one by one until we get our restoration complete. Rabbi Simon is of the priestly family born to help his people.

The Kohen is meant to be a benefit to the people of Y'sra'el and is one of the person's that has been given the authority to stand between the heavenly court and the earthly realm. Christian clergy has been lying to you for so long that you don't know what is good for you anymore. The Melekzadek priest's job is not to stand between the heaven and earth as you have been wrongly taught, his job is to be a King and serve justice on the earth with the Torah. While the Christian clergy teaches everyone can be Melekzadek this is not the truth. Only the Kings of Israel can right hold that title, its not for anyone else.

There is only one everlasting priesthood and that is the Lewitical one. This book has been written by a Lewitical priest of Beyth of Tzadok, its time you reap the benefits so decide wisely. Even if you are a gentile looking to become part of Israel by conversion the opportunity is open to you to obey the Torah.

I want you all to benefit and to receive what rightly belongs to you.

This book for $100 a piece because everything in this manual would forever change your life once you put it in practice but I decided not to do that as my purpose was not that.

However this book is kept at a low price not for $100, no, not even $50 but for a price of $27 only this will forever change the way you think and pray. I am practically giving this away for you to better your lives. The rest is up to you.

Seferim Khanok

New releases for 2015/2016/2017
Ancient Hebrew – Functions, Methods and Meanings. Where did we go wrong?

Religious Confusion and the Everlasting Path to Torah
All the myriads of religious denominations and religious quagmire out there and why the paths of the Torah are the only paths to success and happiness with everlasting life.

www.ingramcontent.com/pod-product-compliance
Lightning Source LLC
Chambersburg PA
CBHW031313150426
43191CB00005B/207